BEYOND THE UNIFORM

A CAREER TRANSITION GUIDE FOR VETERANS AND FEDERAL EMPLOYEES

W. DEAN LEE

JOHN WILEY & SONS, INC.
New York • Chichester • Brisbane • Toronto • Singapore

Copyright © 1991 by John Wiley & Sons, Inc.

All rights reserved. Published simultaneously in Canada.

Reproduction or translation of any part of this work
beyond that permitted by Section 107 or 108 of the
1976 United States Copyright Act without the permission
of the copyright owner is unlawful. Requests for
permission or further information should be addressed to
the Permissions Department, John Wiley & Sons, Inc.

This publication is designed to provide accurate and
authoritative information in regard to the subject
matter covered. It is sold with the understanding that
the publisher is not engaged in rendering legal, accounting,
or other professional service. If legal advice or other
expert assistance is required, the services of a competent
professional person should be sought. *From a Declaration
of Principles jointly adopted by a Committee of the
American Bar Association and a Committee of Publishers.*

Library of Congress Cataloging in Publication Data:

Lee, W. Dean, 1957–
    Beyond the uniform / by W. Dean Lee.
      p. cm.
    Includes index.
    ISBN 0-471-54620-8
    1. Job hunting—United States. 2. Résumés (Employment) 3. Retired
military personnel—Employment—United States.   4. Career changes—
United States. I. Title.
HF5382.75.U6L43 1991
650.14′024355—dc20   91-7768

Printed in the United States of America
10 9 8 7 6 5 4 3 2 1

To my family,
whose silent sacrifices will always
inspire me to magnificent new heights.

And to all soldiers, sailors,
airmen, and marines,
whose gallant sacrifices
will always keep our America free.

ABOUT THE AUTHOR

W. Dean Lee has earned degrees in psychology and sociology, and is an alumnus of numerous institutions for advanced leadership and management. He commenced his national service as a Distinguished Military Graduate.

During his watch as a Regular Army Commissioned Officer, he completed eight tours of duty and logged over 100,000 TDY miles. Missions have taken him from Arctic tundra to desert sands, from computer center to SCIF, and from the classroom to the DMZ. He has held a variety of positions in the infantry and special forces, including commander, leader, principal staff officer, director, instructor, and advisor. His assignments extend to service in administration, intelligence, operations, logistics, foreign areas, and special operations. Mr. Lee's most recent military assignment was commanding officer of a 318-soldier company in a basic combat training task force. Among his awards are three Achievement Medals, three Commendation Medals, and two Meritorious Service Medals.

Mr. Lee is now continuing his journey as an operations advisor and technical analyst.

ACKNOWLEDGMENTS

As we voyage beyond, our legacies will be reflected in the deeds we perform, the images we create, the followers we inspire. This book is part of my living legacy to the future. However, it would not have been possible without some wonderful and caring people whose lasting contributions to my life will be forever remembered and cherished.

Among these inspirational leaders are *SFC Robert Warren*, my original platoon sergeant, for teaching me about the "other side" of real leadership; *MAJ Drew D. Dix* (famed Congressional Medal of Honor recipient), for asking me, as F-4 Phantoms rolled in for a final strafe, "Well L.T., what do you want to do next?" and than making my request a reality; *MAJ Ronald H. Harrison*, a cool-headed "snake eater" with his magical rucksack of tips on survival and tradecraft; and *CPT Alan H. Maestas*, for keeping me out of classified hot waters.

Included for accolades are the die-hard members of the "scorpion team" and our prairie pathfinders, *MAJ Don P. Dickinson*, an expert serpent master, for granting me the maximum freedom in getting the job done; and *LTC Robert S. Henderson*, a celestial navigator of the desert, for guiding me away from many terminating traps.

My gratitude to the "special operators" in my life: *CPT Whitney J. Robinson*, an esteemed friend and "total professional," his lovely wife *Elaine*, and their children *William* and *Daniel*, for all their support and care; *MAJ Cary W. Studley*, an authentic "BUDs" man, for his faithful dependability; *COL David J. Baratto*, the eagle, for letting me "take the ball and run with it"; *LTC John P. Gritz*, for the invitation to advance; and *LTC Robert K. Suchke*, for his superb words of recommendations.

I am indebted to the countless hardworking NCOs wearing steel pots, campaign hats, and berets who are the true heroes in my career; to *1SG Michael D. Shea*, the ultimate "top sergeant," for keeping the company and me squared away; *Mrs. Judy Shea*, for her years of selfless devotion to the medical community; *1SG Joaquin A. Kiyoshi*, a great first sergeant, for keeping everything and everyone combat ready; *Mrs. J. Kiyoshi*, for her support to our "company family"; *CPT Henry J. Sienkiewicz* and *lLT Augustus V. Mataban*, the dedicated "X.O.s" who actually did all the hard work; and *LTC* and *Mrs. Michael J. McKean*, for taking care of our soldiers.

Sincere recognition goes to *CPT Stephen Noyes*, for his "airborne" connection and assistance; *CPT and Mrs. Alan J. Probst*, for their insightful suggestions; *LTC Richard L. Rutledge* and *LTC Thomas F. Page*, for their words of endorsement; *BG and Mrs. David E.K. Cooper*, for their bolstering support; and *MG James W. Wurman*, for his thoughtful comments.

More recently, I appreciate the support of *Ms. Cathy L. Thornton*, a special young lady with a beautiful heart full of cheer and optimism; *Mr. Tony Lee*, the newspaper editor that gave me the "Wall Street" exposure; *Mr. Michael J. Hamilton*, the senior editor, for taking the risk in sponsoring this novice writer; *Ms. Mary Daniello*, for orchestrating this production; and especially, *Ms. Martha M. Urban*, the talented copy editor for her invaluable assistance.

Finally, my deepest gratitude goes to the entire *Lee Family*, both near and far, for their years of quiet love and enduring strength.

NOTE: These important people in my life are listed chronologically, as our paths crossed. Many have since been twice promoted and/or retired; all are continuing their success by blazing new trails for others to follow.

W.D.L.

CONTENTS

INTRODUCTION

Marching into the future as a civilian again can be a marvelous new adventure or a terrifying trauma. After years of dedicated service to the nation, you must now reorient your goals. The longer your service, the more difficult it may be for you to accept the impending changes in your life. Fortunately, your and your family's preparedness now can significantly reduce the stresses that will undoubtedly increase as your day of discharge approaches.

   Within the finite boundaries of these book covers can be found the infinite possibilities for future success. Assembled here is an accumulation of knowledge and experience about the world of modern career transition, captured and condensed to help you avoid the pitfalls of unawareness as you build your new career. Whether you wear a uniform or a business suit, the principles and suggestions are equally valid. The text provides down-to-earth usable information to ease your transition from battle dress uniform (BDU) to pinstriped suit. Although this text was written with the new veteran in mind, more than 90 percent of the details will be useful to any new job seeker, whether civilian or governmental employee. Critical insights are also provided to help family members better understand and prepare for this crucial and often perplexing time.

1

There are no guarantees for instant success. But you will find an abundance of practical information and encouragement to help you conquer what will probably be one of the most difficult challenges you may ever encounter. The worst threat is fear of the unknown. Remember the ancient but dependable dictum: Knowledge is power. Those who possess it have the keys to their future.

Regardless of whether you are a discharged soldier, sailor, airman, or marine, an officer or noncommissioned officer, or a former federal employee, your status is the same: Civilian for Hire. Book stores are full of how-to books written for civilians, by civilians. This book is unique and personal, written for military professionals by a concerned professional officer. It goes well beyond mere résumé-writing and job-interviewing tips; it provides an array of balanced ideas and suggestions to guide you throughout the transition process.

From the youngest private to the oldest general, from mail room clerk to senior executive, everyone eventually develops a quasi-plan for changing careers. Naturally some will be more successful than others. Those who assimilate information and ideas easily and quickly will be the best prepared.

Many veterans have traveled this route before and discovered the same traps and pitfalls. Unfortunately, once their journey was completed, they became immersed in the day-to-day realities of new careers and forgot the horrors of yesterday. Because their valuable lessons were not passed on, others were doomed to experience the same ordeals and struggles.

My goal is to forewarn and prevent you from making the same mistakes and from falling prey to many hidden traps. A great amount of information is available, but you need to put it together and make it work for you. To stay in front of the proverbial power curve, begin your preparation today.

Find a quiet place for your headquarters, a location where you can routinely go each morning to conduct your research. Ideally it should be a place with a telephone, outside calling access codes, a copier, word processor, stationery supplies, fax machine, and answering machine; an office to use as your central business address where potential employers could directly contact you. It should not be a place to socialize with old buddies.

Scan this book with an open mind to capture its essence. Then savor the fine details over the course of two or three days. Avoid subjecting yourself to information overload. Highlight important passages and write in the margins to improve your comprehension and retention. Urge your family to read this book.

If you have already started your research, you probably have discovered what a tremendous amount of information is available, information that you had to search for in many different places, determine what was useful, and organize to suit your needs. Finally, you had to apply it successfully. Too often much valuable time and energy were wasted trying to fit the pieces of the puzzle together.

That was the impetus for developing this book: to find a better solution to this puzzle. By providing an organized set of step-by-step procedures for efficiently and effectively completing your search mission, this guide can save you hundreds of hours of time, keep you from being overwhelmed by extraneous data, and guide you through one of life's most frustrating mazes.

This book is the product of many months of extensive research, including reading the pertinent literature, gleaning ideas from professionals, and recording the experiences of friends who had already traveled this route. Many lessons were learned through old-fashioned trial and error and a series of real-life misadventures. You can avoid repeating the mistakes of others by applying the lessons shared here.

Despite continuing conflicts in the world, major force reductions are ongoing and still a legitimate concern for military personnel. Ironically, not long ago the thought of massive numbers of Americans and allied forces in the Persian Gulf region was only a scenario on paper. Now it is history, underscoring the unpredictability of life. So celebrate your glory days while you can. For this moment in time, your destiny belongs to you.

Make the transition to civilian life as easy as possible. Enjoy a relaxing hobby. Find a diversion to maintain your sanity and fill the void on your résumé between military and civilian employment. Prepare yourself for an agonizingly long wait. It will be punctuated by many moments of inactivity between busy periods spent dispatching résumés, responding to job ads, researching potential employers, preparing for interviews, and writing follow-up letters. Finally, you must steel yourself to wait months for the "right offer."

Many experts say to anticipate waiting one month for every $10,000 you expect in salary. Others, less optimistic, warn: one week for every $1,000. Generally, the higher your salary goal, the more intense your search must be, and the longer you may have to endure before receiving an acceptable offer. Plan on the possibility that it could take over one year to locate a permanent position, perhaps even longer to reach your salary goal. You will learn later how a host of factors will influence your waiting time.

Continue your odyssey by reading ahead. Save yourself from unnecessary and costly mistakes. Your adventure to a new life begins with your first steps. And now to the first chapter.

THE TRIBE

A FAMILY EFFORT

Your family is your life. From this moment on, involve your entire family in the planning and decision-making process. As you begin your search for a new career, don't try to carry the weight of the future alone. Your family's emotional support is essential to your good mental and physical health. If you are single, try to rely on close friends and relatives. Family and friends are your ultimate security dome for the present and future.

The more years you served, the more ingrained the military life-style has become, and the more difficult it may be for your family to adjust to civilian life. These burdens of transition must be equally shared, as your family has probably already realized. Let them help; they can be your pillars of strength. Solid family support makes coping with hardships a little easier and can lead to stronger familial bonds. You will discover that you are going to need each other more than ever during this critical period of adjustment.

Remember, your feelings, attitudes, and behaviors are infectious. Your anxieties and frustrations, whether expressed or concealed, will be reflected by your spouse and children. Be conscious of their genuine emotions and the accumulated effects of despair. In Chapter 2, "A Psychodrama," a series of topics will be presented to help you and your family anticipate, understand, and cope with this temporary predicament. Helping you confront your troubles should help ease their fears.

As you progress in life, so must your family. If you are planning to resettle, remember that your spouse may also be searching for a new job. Excellent sources of job information will be presented in Chapter 10, "Networking." Consolidate your efforts and transform the job hunt into an educational and pleasurable adventure. You can assist each other by sharing such responsibilities as researching company information, critiquing interview rehearsals, scheduling appointments, answering telephones, chauffeuring, baby-sitting, and giving each other encouragement.

SHARING THE ADVENTURE

Consider taking your family along as you travel to distant cities for interviews. While you are interviewing, your family could be checking out the area's housing and schools. Exchange information in the evening while enjoying a family dinner and a little sight-seeing.

During this planning phase, discuss where your family will stay while you job hunt. Will they stay with you in a temporary apartment? Live out of your station wagon? In a new motor home? Or will they stay with parents, in-laws, or friends? What will you do with your pets? The advantageous and disadvantageous of family togetherness, expenses and money worries, and the frustrations of long travel—all need to be openly discussed.

A very important consideration is where your children will attend school. Your planned summer search may become a yearlong ordeal. Compromise on what you think is best for your children and what will make your family the happiest.

IDENTIFYING YOUR OPTIONS

To identify your options, examine your financial resources. Chapter 3, "The Means," provides an easy method for itemizing your assets. Review your family's insurance program. The gap between military coverage, Civilian Health & Medical Program of the Uniformed Services (CHAMPUS), and your future employer's program may be unpredictable. Useful information about your Servicemen's Group Life Insurance (SGLI) will be offered in Chapter 15, "A Potpourri of Veteran Benefits." Consult with your insurance agent about the various types of coverage plans available and which best suits your requirements. Discuss the needs for temporary and/or long-term medical coverage.

Consider the possibility that your future employer may not provide group disability insurance or may provide inadequate coverage. Recognize your need for personal property insurance to cover household furnishings and special belongings during transit or in storage. Don't let a major illness, injury, or loss devastate your finances.

The United Services Automobile Association (USAA) offers a useful booklet, *Moving With the Military*. A practical guide to help organize your move, it contains useful checklists and tips on how to use available resources. This free booklet can be obtained by calling USAA at 1-800-531-8857.

I cannot emphasize too much the importance of your family's involvement. Enrich their knowledge and experience by sharing with them the information you are learning. At every stage in this endeavor, the family will be the cornerstone of your success.

In the chapters to come, you will be shown how to develop a family plan of action that will realistically project your activities for the next several months. Chapter 5, "Insights," will provide a starting point for identifying and ranking your family's goals. By establishing a series of short-term objectives, you can more confidently pursue your long-term goals. These will become your stepping stones to success.

Your long-term goals will give your family a better perspective of your destination and routes to its achievement. Developing long-term goals promotes needed continuity in your planning efforts. However, you must keep your plan flexible enough to comfortably accommodate unforeseen changes.

Your short-term objectives must be reachable with the resources you have available. Experience has shown that those who successfully reach their objectives, with the minimum amount of stress and time, are those who analyze their resources, plan their future, map out strategies, and conscientiously stick to their plan. A successful plan will improve your mental well-being, employment options, opportunities for success, and overall life satisfaction.

Your first step in the planning process is to refresh your self-awareness and improve your family's future outlook. How to do this is discussed in Chapter 2.

A PSYCHODRAMA

Prepare yourself and your family to wage a cerebral battle. To achieve victory, you must understand your strengths and vulnerabilities. Develop a successful counterstrategy. Instill in yourselves a winning attitude. The more you understand the impending threat to your emotional well-being, the better your defenses will be. Some anxieties are bound to affect you even if you expect to be happily retired or gladly separated.

Our mental processes are probably more predictable than we care to admit. You will experience increased stresses. These are normal occurrences that we all experience at one time or another. The frequency and duration of these stresses will vary with your personality, history, future outlook, self-esteem, family support, environment, and physical health.

STRESS: EARLY WARNING SIGN

Stress can be both beneficial and harmful. Stress can set off feelings of dispair and depression. Stress can also prompt the feelings of exhilaration and ecstasy one feels, say, when free falling at 8,300 feet or rafting down the white rapids of the Colorado. Stress triggers the body's safety mechanism, allowing you to avoid many of life's unplanned dangers—for instance, leaping out of the path of a speeding car or handling emergency crises. Stress can improve your daily productivity, energizing you to meet tight deadlines and deal effectively with tough problems.

Scientists now believe that the amount of stress a person experiences may not necessarily lead to further anxiety and depression. Instead, they are learning that a person's inability to control and handle stressful conditions is the leading culprit.

Your success in staying physically and mentally healthy depends on your ability to identify those stresses that are preventable, avoidable, and controllable. Focus your energies on effectively managing those stresses that you cannot prevent but that you can control.

Harmful stress may not only damage psychologically but manifest itself in a variety of physical signs and symptoms as well. Some of the most common indicators are headaches, neck and back pains, heartburn, stomach pains, nausea, constipation or diarrhea, unusual allergy attacks, skin disorders, and increased susceptibility to infections. Consult with your physician if you are continually plagued with any of these problems. Stress may not be the only cause; these may be early warning signs of other underlying diseases.

The important thing to remember is that most of your reactions are normal. However, what is normal for you depends on how you interpret experience. Stress affects people differently, and even the same pressure will affect a person differently at different times. Some anxieties may not occur; others may occur in different order or intensity. Your family and friends can help alert you to any major behavioral changes that may require outside intervention.

A PERIOD OF TRANSITION

Throughout the transition period, you may experience periods of total sadness and a lack of interest or pleasure in daily life. The following are other feelings you may have and some suggested coping mechanisms.

☐ **Depression.** "I am not a team member any more." Depression is a natural reaction to stress, severe illness, and disability, and is applicable to all veterans and their families. Your vulnerability increases if you are lonely, anxious, cannot forget past mistakes, or a poor problem solver. Early acceptance that you are leaving one team will bring you closer to being a member of a new team.

Think positively about the future, concentrate on new successes, force yourself to drive through adversity, just as you did throughout your service life. Remember, things could be a lot worse; there are hundreds of thousands of people in this world who would be willing to trade places with you. If you are retired, enjoy your well-deserved "freedom."

☐ **Rejection.** "No! This must be a mistake." If you are being involuntarily separated for causes you do not understand, ask your superiors to check. Perhaps you were erroneously placed on the wrong list. If you are absolutely convinced that an injustice was done, use your rights of appeal, review, and reconsideration. At this point, you may have nothing more to lose and a career to retain. Be careful, however; assumption that the rejection is false could be a denial mechanism, whereby you refuse to acknowledge the truth. Government budget reductions are quite real.

☐ **Guilt.** "What did I do wrong?" To those involuntarily discharged, I urge a serious and honest self-examination of your career. You probably know what you did or didn't do to put yourself in this predicament. We all make mistakes; if we are wise, we learn from them and don't repeat them in the future. You may be just another victim of circumstances (for example, budget cutbacks, reduced promotion slots, late advancement opportunities, and so forth).

Relax and take solace that many successful people have made this same passage. For example, owing to a lack of leadership opportunities, General Dwight D. Eisenhower remained a major for 15 years!

☐ **Frustration.** "I worked hard and always did the best I could, but look where it got me!" Frustration is an appropriate reaction for those who are involuntarily separated or requested to retire early. But don't let it make you bitter. If you are a decent and honest worker, be proud of your achievements. Recall the many sacrifices you made, the challenges conquered, the extra effort gladly contributed to our country.

☐ **Anger.** "I gave the service the best years of my life, and this is the thanks I get!" For those who may be the victim of a reduction in force or promotion pass over, anger is natural. However, being or staying angry will only bring you more grief. Be angry for one night, safely release all your rage, and get it over. Consider this transition time as a blessing in disguise, a stepping-stone to greater success. Remember all those times that you asked yourself why you were doing this and thinking that you could do better in civilian life. Well, this is your opportunity to take control of your destiny and make those dreams come true.

☐ **Anxiety.** "What am I going to do now?" You and your spouse will ask yourselves that question time and again until the transition is complete weeks or months from now. By then you will be comfortably settled into your new career, home, and community. In the meantime, your feelings of anxiety may multiply and cripple your thought process unless you come to terms with these feelings early. By recognizing and anticipating periods of anxiety, you can better prevent their negative impact.

Shared Anxieties

Personal problems are infectious; they can quickly spread to your family. Here are some shared anxieties to warn your family to anticipate. Tell them that recognition of these early warning signs is the first step toward a cure.

☐ **Family.** Separation from a military career will affect the entire family. Your spouse may have to change jobs. The family will experience the headaches of another major house move and possibly the inconvenience of a temporary step-down in living conditions. Children will have to leave old friends and schools; the family will lose the social prestige you had attained as an officer or NCO; and the close-knit feelings of living in a military community will be gone.

☐ **Security.** Loss of job security and financial and medical benefits will be difficult to accept at first. But as your new career stabilizes, these benefits should gradually resume. Of course, for those officially retiring, financial and medical benefits are virtually guaranteed.

☐ **Image.** Depending on your self-esteem and what you consider to be truly important in life, you will probably find that your public self-image is only temporarily tarnished. Replacing duty titles is an ongoing process that you will gradually adapt to.

☐ **Rejection shocks.** Be prepared to play out a minipsychodrama every time you receive a letter of rejection. Depending on how many résumés you sent out and how many applications you submitted, you may be in for an emotional roller coaster ride. Keep in mind that the more résumés you send out, the greater your opportunity of being accepted. The feeling of rejection usually subsides after the first dozen rejection letters.

Coping Mechanisms

It is natural for you to occasionally feel lonely, fearful, useless, or desperate, and for your family to experience humiliation, bitterness, and resentment. Prevent erosion of self-confidence and family depression by eliminating your negative time and energies.

☐ **Count your blessings.** Stop wallowing in self-pity. Start looking at life optimistically. Remember, positive and enthusiastic people attract the same. You are alive, healthy, have a future and the freedom to influence it!

☐ **Believe in yourself.** Have faith that everything will work out, sooner or later, for better or for worse. By learning from the hard times in your life, you achieve a better appreciation of the good times.

☐ **Be good to yourself.** If you follow popular advice and conduct a grueling seven-day-a-week job hunt, you may be setting yourself up for early failure, a potential victim of burnout. Prevent self-inflicted stresses by dedicating one or two days to relaxing, recharging your internal batteries, and just enjoying your family. Your renewed energies and spirits will allow you to be more focused and productive in your job search. Take good care of yourself because you will have to live with yourself for the rest of your life.

☐ **Think positive.** Positive "vibrations" are contagious. Surround yourself with cheerful and optimistic people.

☐ **Exercise.** Extra physical activity will reduce your tensions and anxieties; increase your strength, stamina, and vitality. It will also improve your appearance for your interviews. Just as you did in the service, develop a physical training (PT) schedule, with some activity scheduled for every other day, and force yourself to do it. Turn PT into family fun projects of bicycling, jogging, or swimming. Think about joining a sports club.

☐ **Set family goals.** Make a family schedule of specific daily goals, goals that are achieveable, measurable, useful and, preferably, fun. A series of small, easily obtainable goals will be more beneficial than one large hard-to-achieve dream. Family projects could include cleaning out the garage or painting the bathroom. Turn keep-busy work into productive challenges.

☐ **Review daily accomplishments.** Each night, as you see physical progress being made, your morale will improve, self-confidence build, and family esteem strengthen.

☐ **Use free time constructively.** Consider using free time to pursue other interests that will both constructively occupy your mind and benefit your future. For example, you could take a few college courses to improve your education credentials and enhance your marketability. Seriously consider enrolling in a usable foreign language or computer literacy course.

☐ **Share your talents.** Volunteer your talents to help your community and reinforce your networking assets. Be a temporary consultant to fill the unemployment gap in your résumé. Participating in civilian community organizations and church groups will also help you feel more at home in your new community.

☐ **Stay healthy.** Eat a balanced diet of nutritional foods. Keep your body properly fueled to handle the increased mental stress and likelihood of decreased physical activity. Be extra cautious of excessive weight gains or losses in you or your spouse. Uncontrolled overeating or unnecessary dieting are inappropriate responses that may lead to other physical and emotional problems. Good food and regular mealtimes are essential for replenishing your body's requirement for vital nutrients.

☐ **Sleep well.** Maintain a regular sleeping schedule. Sleep is nature's time to heal your mind, body, and spirits. Whether you find a series of daily naps or a nightly period of long, deep sleep more beneficial, give yourself this opportunity to rest, repair, and refresh. Sleep improves your alertness, enhances the assimilation and retention of information, reduces irritability and temper flares, and helps you maintain a sense of humor.

☐ **Get away from it all.** If you reach a point of total frustration, consider taking a short retreat from daily worries. Objectively examine your life, your personal interests, your lifelong objectives, your family needs and desires, and what makes you really happy.

When to Seek Professional Help

Remember when you were in charge and helped all those people through counseling? Or if they had serious problems, how you referred them to more knowledgeable experts? There is no shame in seeking professional assistance. It is better to deal with minor annoyances now rather than let them inflate into major problems later. A final comment about depression.

It is absolutely natural to occasionally feel blue, but when it does not stop, it is time to seek professional help. Each person will exhibit different signs of despair and varying intensities of melancholy.

A prolonged, deep depression is a serious disease, but it is treatable. Do not ignore these warning signs:

Persistent melancholia

Long-term sadness

Constant troublesome thoughts

Feelings of complete hopelessness, unworthiness, or guilt

Loss of overall pleasure and enjoyment in life

Cessation of laughing and smiling

Chronic fidgetiness, uneasiness, or restlessness

Eating disorders: carbohydrate craving, significant weight gains or losses

Impaired thinking and memory

Indecisive decision making

Low energy levels

Sleeping disorders: trouble getting to sleep, excessive sleeping, unexplained interruptions, frequent bizarre nightmares, no memory of dreaming, and difficulty in getting out of bed

Dramatic mood swings

Constant thoughts of death and self-destruction

Discuss your condition with your physician. Your doctor may recommend a family counselor. A few therapy sessions may be sufficient to resolve the problem. If the problem is more severe, a psychiatrist may prescribe the temporary use of beneficial medication. To avoid tragedy, anyone experiencing continual thoughts of suicide must seek immediate professional care.

Compel yourself to relax mentally and stay physically healthy. Listen to some music, read a good book, watch a comedy show, have a good dinner, enjoy your family, take it easy, and enjoy your life.

THE ART OF MENTAL RELAXATION

Try this popular, safe, simple, and relatively effective psychic exercise. It may help you regain your tranquility and peace of mind. Try it a few times to see if it works for you.

Find a quiet place to meditate in solitude. Select a secluded place in your home or office, away from any distractions. Demand not to be disturbed for about 10 minutes. Or go hide in the car. If you like, play a tape of some gentle soothing background music.

Sit in the middle of your bed, or on a cushioned carpet or soft ground. Sit with your legs crossed, whether Indian or yoga style is unimportant, just as long as you are comfortable. If you are not used to field sitting or are physically unable, sit in a comfortable high-back chair.

Prevent any personal injuries by carefully removing all hazardous objects that you may accidentally come in contact with.

Now to begin the exercise. Let your head naturally droop slightly forward, or let it relax on the headrest of the chair. Keep your back straight to improve your breathing. Place your open palms in your lap. If your are in a chair, plant your feet firmly on the ground. Then just let all the muscles in your body relax.

Close your eyes. Visualize being in a peaceful and serene place—perhaps sitting beside a small placid lake, or in a tranquil green meadow during the autumn season. Or imagine yourself peacefully gazing up at the brilliant stars of a clear spring night. This is your fantasy and you control the scenery.

Mentally picture some pleasant surroundings, images that make you feel restful. As you look at different parts of your scene, gradually begin to focus the images upon yourself.

Gently, but deeply, inhale through your mouth and slowly exhale through your nose. Pause a few seconds with each breath. Listen to your own natural rhythms. Let your body take control.

As you sit in your imaginary world of absolute harmony, use your mind's eye to see each part of your body relaxing. Start with your hair and relax down to your toes. As you let out each breath, feel that part of your body relaxing.

Mentally visualize and physically feel each muscle relaxing as your inner tension dissolves away. Continue these thoughts and feelings until your entire body is pacified.

When you have completed this exercise, your whole body should be relaxed, your mind clear. You should emerge with renewed spirits and a feeling of calmness and self-control. If you discover yourself waking up from a short nap, that is fine; you probably needed the refreshing sleep anyway. That was the purpose of those earlier precautions about removing any hazardous objects, so that if you fell over you would not hurt yourself.

It may take a few attempts to become accustomed to this routine, but mastery depends on you and your willingness to temporarily surrender control of your body. Although it sounds exotic and far-fetched, this is a no-cost, low-thrill mental exercise for your mind, one that is possibly as beneficial to your well-being as that afternoon run is to your heart, lungs, and body.

All the wealth and wisdom of the world may not bring you inner peace and self-contentment. But inner peace and self-contentment could lead you to greater wealth and wisdom.

Now back to work. To help confront your money fears and chart your financial fortune, some capital suggestions are offered in the next chapter.

CHAPTER 3

THE MEANS

THE IMPORTANCE OF MONEY

If you are independently wealthy and have an endless money supply, you may disregard this chapter. But if you are like the rest of us paycheck-to-paycheck survivors, the number one suggestion for you is to start saving money now. If you have already started saving, outstanding; save some more! Congratulation to those retiring with a pension, you earned it and deserve to enjoy the better things in life. But you, too, must continue to keep a small reserve just in case of the unexpected; many experts recommend having enough money in reserve to cover living expenses for at least six months.

The importance of financial security cannot be overemphasized. It will make a tremendous difference in your whole attitude and approach to a job search. It will mean the difference between struggling for existence and living comfortably.

The greater your cash reserve, the greater your control of your destiny. Money will buy you the luxury of more time to carefully evaluate the direction of your career and to select the best job offer. You will also be in a better bargaining position to negotiate a higher

19

salary because your potential employer will realize you are not desperate for a paycheck and willing to accept the first low salary offer.

Be cautions about accepting the first job offer just to have money coming in or something to do. You may find yourself quickly dissatisfied and eventually quit, or even be fired. Then you will have to start the search process over again. But do not ignore that first offer, it may be the only one for several months.

MONEY CONSERVATION PLAN

To prepare yourself for the long haul, develop a money conservation plan. Here is how to start.

☐ **Step 1: Itemize assets.** Itemize all your financial assets. List all usable income—money that you have immediate access to. Also list all potential cash sources, such as items you plan to sell to help build up your cash reserve. Unless you are sincerely able to part company with one of your valuable possessions, do not list it as a usable asset; you will only be inflating the amount of your available funds.

☐ **Step 2: Calculate interim income.** Calculate how much additional income you will accumulate between now and the date of your separation. Include future paychecks, accruing bank interest, pay from moonlighting jobs, your spouse's pay, and any monetary gifts from your parents. Remember to include any entitled separation pay.

To simplify completing steps 1 and 2, turn to Appendix A, "Means Calculation," and use the handy form Sources of Monthly Income. Before filling it out, make several copies for future use.

At the time of this writing, the politicians and "purple suitors" were devising different payment schemes for involuntarily separated service members. One suggestion was to pay both involuntarily separated officers and enlisted personnel one lump-sum payment, without any monetary ceiling. This figure is calculated by taking 10 percent of your current basic pay and multiplying it by your total number of service years. Keep in mind that this was only one proposal that was gaining popular acceptance.

Presently only involuntarily separated commissioned officers with more than six years of service are eligible for separation pay. (Officers commissioned before November 5, 1985, are eligible after serving only five years.) The maximum that currently may be paid is $30,000, less 20 percent for federal taxes, leaving you with $24,000. By the time you read this, the boys in Washington may have "changed" the truth. Check with your finance office for updated changes and revised pay formulas.

Fortunately all service members still have the option to "cash in" their accrued leave. Exchanging leave days for cash is a good option to consider if your cash reserve is low. Important words of caution: 20 percent of any amount received will be immediately deducted for federal taxes. Also, only a maximum of 60 accrued leave days can be cashed in. Keep that in mind as you and your family decide whether to take terminal leave or make an advance cash exchange. By taking terminal leave near the end of your tour, you continue to receive active duty pay, allowances, insurance coverage, and travel benefits.

To figure out how much you are entitled to for a leave cash-in, get out your last Leave and Earnings Statement (LES) and follow along:

Determine how many leave days you *will* have accrued by your separation day. Do not forget to subtract any leave days you will use between now and separation.

Total the number of days you will cash in.

Divide one month's basic pay by 30.

Multiply the result by the total number of cashed in days.

Subtract 20 percent for taxes.

The remainder is the total amount you should receive.

☐ **Step 3: Itemize monthly expenses.** Make a list of all of your expenditures for an average month. A good technique is to review all receipts for the past year. To help you compute the numbers, see the Monthly Expenses form in Appendix A.

If your are presently living on post or base, remember that you will be losing many often-unrealized benefits and inheriting new civilian expenses. Here is a small sample of costs to expect on the "outside": mortgage, rent, property taxes, insurance, association fees, electricity, gas, water, sewage, trash collection, higher grocery and shopping bills.

Do not hit the panic button. Just remember that hundreds of thousands of civilians with half your present income and savings are making it, and you will too. Sure it's going to be a bit rough at first, but think of the millions of successful foreign immigrants who came to our country with nothing more than a pocketful of dreams. Recalling their successes can help sustain you during your dark phases.

Another major expenditure to consider is increased taxes. This applies especially to those receiving separation pay. That windfall may turn into a financial nightmare unless you wisely put aside for your next very hefty tax bill.

If you are one of the many thousands who declared legal residency in a nontaxing state while you were serving around the globe, remember you will cease to be protected under the Soldiers & Sailors Relief Act. Expect to begin paying state real estate and income taxes wherever you decide to establish your home and career. Keep that in mind as you and your family study the atlas in search of a low- or nontaxing state.

☐ **Step 4: Analyze monthly expenditures.**   Scrutinize your list of expenditures. Examine your life-style and spending patterns. As a family, decide which items are essential, which represent creature comforts, and which are luxuries. The forms in Appendix A can be useful here.

Remember what was said earlier about the family's sharing the burdens of responsibility; tightening the money belt is a critical part of that. Squabbles over money matters can be avoided if everyone understands their financial obligations up front.

All unnecessary expenses should be eliminated. Curtail any major purchases until after you have settled into your new career. If you receive separation pay, you may be tempted to go out and splurge. Truthfully ask yourself if you really can afford to buy right now and how much can you spend. If your planned budget allows, you might be wise to stock up on lower cost essential products from the exchange and commissary. Guard against overstocking, especially if you plan to make a major do-it-yourself (DITY) move. Also remember that you will be paying for additional expenses if you exceed your authorized weight allowances.

Many decide to take a vacation and enjoy themselves while they are still on Uncle Sam's payroll; to have some fun before facing the dreaded chore of looking for a new job. This can be time and money wasted, because of constant worry about what is going to happen after the vacation. Others find it more enjoyable and fun to take a vacation after their new contract is signed and before they report for their first civilian workday.

If you decide to do some globe-trotting while you still have military Airlift Command (MAC) flight privileges, beware of long waits at terminals, cancelled connections, delayed flights, and the possiblity of having to return by commercial airliner. Such an adventure may prove more costly in valuable time and money than you expect unless, of course, you have a large amount of excess leave and prearranged cash to use.

Depending on your personality, you might find a short sabbatical helpful for clearing the mind, reassessing your priorities, and rejuvenating your energy. The secret is to keep it short and inexpensive; you will need the saved time and money later. Try a quick holiday of relaxation at a local resort.

Avoid living in self-imposed poverty or a fantasy world of inaction because "they'll soon be breaking down the door to hire me." Remember your dreams; use your money as stepping-stones to success.

If you have not caught on by now, this task of listing your assets and liabilities is not just a mental drill. It was designed to give you and your family a chance to work and come together. By now everyone should have a better understanding of where the money has been going and where it should go in the future. You should also have a good idea of how much money you will have set aside in your reserve fund.

☐ **Step 5: Determine net assets.**   From your total of present and future assets, subtract all present and future liabilities (use the Balance Sheet in Appendix A). This should give you a good idea of what your reserve capital will be. Compare this amount with what you estimate your future temporarily jobless and frugal life-style will cost. Now you can calculate how long you can survive before your next paycheck. The greater your cash reserve and the fewer your expenses during the transition, the less money worries will distract from your job search.

HIGH COST OF CIVILIAN LIVING

You will be amazed at the high cost of living in the civilian economy, especially if you been used to making the majority of your purchases at the exchange and the commissary. Depending on the area of the country you initially settle in, living expenses may cause culture shock.

Out-of-pocket expenses involved in a job search will be dramatically more than you anticipated. The following is a sample of those hidden costs you can expect to have to pay.

☐ **Transportation expenses.** Higher gasoline bills await you because of increased travel to libraries to conduct research and to potential employers for job interviews and tours. House hunting near your new workplace will also use up gas. Associated car usage fees, such as highway and bridge tolls and very expensive parking fees in the big cities, are other unanticipated expenses. And, if you are planning to move across country to settle down, plan to pay for a complete car servicing and tire replacement.

☐ **Résumé preparation and associated expenses.** A word processor is indispensable during a job search. If you do not already have one, I strongly encourage an early purchase. You will eventually need one to prepare your customized résumés for different companies. Best to buy it now and save yourself the later agony of having to make an unplanned purchase or learn to use it under stress. (More about résumés and word processors later.) You will also need stationery products such as business-quality typing paper for your personalized letters of introduction and customized résumés, business and mailing envelopes, and hundreds of postage stamps. Finally, use of fax machines and overnight mailing services to rush vital information to the prospective employers does not come cheap. These expenses need to be planned for.

☐ **Personal expenses.** You will need new suits, shirts, ties, and shoes for those all-important first-impression job interviews. Also, don't forget the cost of overnight motel accommodations while waiting for interviews, visiting companies, and house hunting; and meals consumed on the road and at those special business lunches with prospective bosses. An answering machine at home and/or office to record job-related messages while you are on the road is a smart buy.

Do exercise good taste in recording your greeting message; remember, the next caller may be your new boss. Another useful tool is a videotape recorder to rehearse your interviews. You can save money by borrowing one or by using an inexpensive pocket tape recorder.

As you can see, the expenses will quickly start to accumulate. Plan to reserve about $5,000 just to cover business expenses alone. Obviously, some people will spend more or less, depending on their life-style, the amount of traveling they are willing to do, the quality of their résumé presentations, and the length of time required to complete their transition.

Flip to Appendix A. The Estimated Monthly Transition Costs form can be used to figure transition costs. Make several copies of this form. At the end of each month, annotate your actual expenses. This then becomes an excellent record for your taxes.

MANAGING DURING THE TRANSITION

When your paycheck stops, so does your scheduled allotments. Develop a new payment plan to handle your mortgage bills, car payments, insurance bills, automatic investments, contributions, and other monthly deductions. Contact those companies and arrange suitable payment methods. Consult with potential employers to see if they will offer you any similar allotment and direct-deposit programs.

Lump-Sum Payment

If you are fortunate to receive any sizable compensation, discuss with your family how to invest or spend it. Remember the large tax payment you will be making next year.

Until you have secured a new and reliable source of regular income, be ultracautious in your financial planning. You want to insure maximum protection of your principal assets, while still retaining quick accessibility.

Be extra vigilant during your transition. This is your window of vulnerability, the time when you are most likely to fall victim to any one of hundreds of disreputable, quick money-making schemes. Some may be so sophisticated and innocent appearing that you may not know you were swindled until weeks or months later. Remember the old maxim: if it's too good to be true, it probably is.

Always consult with a reputable financial manager and tax planner about the best investment strategy for you.

The Tax Angle

Words for the tax wise. Your tax liability may substantially increase during your separation year, especially if you are single, have large taxable interest or dividend income, have few tax deductions, or receive another large windfall (for example, an inheritance, winning a contest, or investment profits). A lump-sum payment combined with your accumulated basic salary and interest from maturing investments may send you soaring into a higher tax bracket.

To reduce next year's tax bill, determine the feasibility of investing some of your uncommitted money into long-term investments such as 18-month certificates of deposit (CDs) or U.S. Treasury notes in the year *prior* to receiving your lump-sum payment. The objective is to reduce your taxable income during the year of discharge. Try to defer the taxable interest to the following year, when you will most likely be receiving less income, especially if you are retiring or still job hunting. This simple technique may dramatically reduce your tax bill and save you thousands of dollars in taxes.

Before investing early or committing any money, carefully research if this strategy is appropriate for you. Use this year's tax tables and rates as a guide for comparing your tax liability with and without the additional effects of maturing investments. Remember, if you elect to park your cash in long-term reserves, your immediate liquidity is reduced and you must be prepared to pay a possibly sizable penalty for any early withdrawal. Plan to invest only that amount that you are certain will not be needed during the term of your investment and transition.

Financial Management

As you begin your new civilian life, be initially conservative with your assets, at least until you are secure in your new profession. Then explore new investment options such as short-term CDs, mutual funds, and high-yield money markets.

Glean ideas and information by reading some of the many financial magazines available: *Money, Business Week, Fortune*, and *Forbes*. Consider reading *Sylvia Porter's Your Finances in the 1990s* written by, you guessed it, Sylvia Porter. This excellent book provides sound advice for building a personal financial plan, investing your capital, creating a children's education fund, and much more.

If safety of principal is your primary concern, consider purchasing U.S. Treasury securities. Like old reliable U.S. savings bonds, these government securities represent an investment in our country's future.

Treasury bills (T-bills) are short-term securities that mature in three months, six months, or one year. They are sold at a discount, which means you purchase them at face value minus the interest. Upon maturity, they are redeemed at full face value. The smallest denomination available is $10,000.

Treasury notes are intermediate securities that mature in from 1 to 10 years. Short-term notes can be purchased in minimum denominations of $5,000 and mature in 4 years or less. The longer term issues are available in denominations of $1,000 and up.

Treasury bonds are long-term investments that mature in from 10 to 40 years. The minimum denomination for a Treasury bond is $1,000.

As you may have surmised, longer term investments require less capital. The interest on U.S. Treasury securities is exempt from state and local income taxes. This advantage will boost your total yield, especially if you live in a high-tax state. These investments are risk free because they are backed by the federal government.

Treasury bills, notes, and bonds are available at any Federal Reserve Bank or branch. Contact your bank for the location of the nearest federal bank, then request their next auction date and projected yields. Treasury issues are also available at most commercial banks, but be prepared to pay the bank a commission of from $25 to $50.

Albeit the selection is yours, consider the safety of your investment, penalties for early withdrawal, ease of access and liquidity, and the safeguards offered by federally insured banking institutions. If you decide to purchase speculative stocks, do not invest more than you are willing to lose. Follow the farmer's advice: don't put all your eggs in one basket.

To offset potential investment hazards, distribute your assets in

several different instruments. By diversifying your investment portfolio among CDs, mutual funds, money markets, government securities, and corporate stocks and bonds, you can safeguard your
financial state. Thus no one single calamity in a conglomerate, enterprise, or market can leave you in a desperate strait.

You want to create a personalized portfolio to meet your unique
investment objectives. Carefully consider your tolerance for taking
monetary risks, especially now that your future is somewhat uncertain. Evaluate your immediate and future needs, tax liabilities, and
mandatory investment holding periods.

When you become firmly situated in your new career and life-style,
your financial situation should improve. Then you will have greater
flexibility to pursue higher returns from growth investments. While
offering higher yields, these funds are less stable and carry a higher
degree of risk.

If you are planning to retire completely, you may want to rebalance
your portfolio to include a higher percentage of stable income pro-
ducers. Seek investment opportunities that are lower in risk, yet still
sufficient to supplement your pension and social security payments.

Discuss your financial objectives with a reputable certified financial
manager, tax planner, or accountant. As your life-style changes, your
investment objectives may have to be readjusted, along with your
investment strategies and portfolio.

Unemployment Compensation

Some words about unemployment pay. Imagining yourself standing
in the unemployment line may not help your self-image and ego, but
neither should losing thousands of dollars of *your* money. Unemployment pay is not charity or welfare money. It is your justified
compensation of mandatory insurance money paid by all employers
to assist financially during these transitions. Unemployment compensation is taxable income. Because federal employers provide additional contributions, you, with your newly acquired veteran's status,
will receive extra compensation.

The registration requirements, entitled compensations, and duration of eligibility varies from state to state. Current federal law limits
veterans to collecting a weekly entitlement of up to $225 for a max-

imum period of 13 weeks. Interestingly, civilians are eligible for up to 26 weeks. As of this writing, Congress is considering lifting the 13-week restriction and permitting the collection of pay one week after discharge. Check with your Veterans Administration counselor for the latest changes.

A simple phone call to the Unemployment Office where you plan to register should answer your questions. You cannot register and collect in different states; this is a one-time offer. If you plan to stay with family or friends during the transition, you would be wise to learn in advance about that state's eligibility rules. These offices are listed in the telephone directory's Blue Pages under the state government's Department of Labor and Unemployment Insurance Compensation Division.

Some requirements are common to most states. For instance, you must have been separated (actual discharge date) a specified minimum time period, usually six weeks, before you are permitted to apply for unemployment pay. On the day you file for unemployment, you must bring proof of your identity (driver's license, reservist red identification card, birth certificate), social security card (or a copy of your LES), your last LES, and your separation papers (DD Form 214), pages 1 and 4.

Expect to wait about one week before receiving your first check. You may have to visit the unemployment office each week to prove that you are still unemployed and actively seeking new employment. Some states may permit you to check in by mail. Some may require you to have visited companies and provide completed Job Seekers Cards to validate that you are actively searching.

If you are an officer or senior NCO seeking a professional management position and relying heavily on résumés and telephone searches, you may be requested to show proof of your weekly mailings in lieu of door-to-door contacts.

Depending on how your state calculates your benefits, you may receive a weekly check for up to one-third of your current LES monthly entitlements. Remember that working for Uncle Sam increases your pay benefits, providing a hefty compensation check that you cannot afford to ignore.

There is no question of swallowing pride. Difficult as it may be to accept now, unemployment compensation is a benefit that you have earned and deserve to receive.

Let me give some final words of encouragement. Eliminate from your mind those embarrassing or humiliating TV scenarios depicting unemployment offices. Most offices are modern looking, efficiently operated, and staffed by empathic professionals.

You will be amazed at the people you may meet in line. By your third visit you probably will have mustered enough courage to remove your sunglasses and park your car closer to the building—just a little humor there. But seriously, do remember to take along all your necessary paper work.

Speaking of paper work, how is your family's bookkeeping system? Read on for some helpful guidance in organizing your business and personal records.

FOR THE RECORD

An accurate and complete record-keeping system will reap you large dividends in time and money. By establishing now and conscientiously maintaining all your records, you can better plan your future and document your past.

TOOLS OF THE TRADE

Establish an organized record-keeping system to direct yourself along the proper transition glide path. The guide markers in the Career Transition Milestones chart will assist you in making an efficient final approach toward landing a new future.

Desk-Top Monthly Planning Calendar

Enter your day of discharge (D-Day) and sequentially number the days before (D − 1, D − 2, . . .) and after (D + 1, D + 2, . . .) it. You're right, this is your new "short-timer's calendar."

CAREER TRANSITION MILESTONES

18–12 Months

Assess goals
  Personal dreams
  Family needs
Identify unified objectives
  Life-style
  Geo-locations
  Education
  Employment
Visit libraries
  Review reading list
  Learn all you can
  Locate reference sources
  Research demographics
Register
  Placement testing
  College admissions
  Aptitude testing
  Trade/language courses
Organize finances
  Consult accountant/planner
  Revise portfolio
  Seek tax-deferred investments
Prepare résumé
  Collect records and reports
  Develop chronology of experience
  Draft résumé
  Complete Form SF-171

12–9 Months

Review résumé
  Obtain professional critique
  Improve and revise
Purchase
  Word processor
  Civilian wardrobe
  Answering machine
Prepare cover letters
  Customize
  Critique and revise
Research
  Business magazines
  Trade journals
  National newspapers
Establish network
  Friends
  Relatives
  Former associates
  Fellow veterans
  New contacts
Start planning calendar
  D-day sequence numbers
  Goal dates
  Important appointments
  Coordination events

9–6 Months

Reassess
  Future goals
  Financial matters
  Résumé contents and appearance
Establish contacts
  Networking assets
  Headhunting firms
  Military associations
Dispatch résumé and cover letters
  Networkers
  Headhunters
  Placement agents
Start daily journal
  Accomplishments
  Important names and addresses
  Significant events
  Follow-up actions
Attend
  Job fair interviews
  Self-help workshops
  Trade and franchise shows
  Transition meetings
Research
  Hidden job market
  Employment newspapers

6–3 Months

Prepare for interviews
  Develop questions and answers
  Rehearse and critique
  Refine presentation
Review periodicals
  Research job ads
  Tailor cover letters and résumés
  Dispatch résumés
  Request company annual reports
Request
  Separation orders
  Letters of recommendation
  Final performance reports
Schedule
  Medical examinations
  Appointments
  Quarters clearing
Organize household goods
  Purchase goods from exchange
  Identify, pack, store, or carry items
Coordinate
  Medical and insurance coverage
  Allotment payments
  Forwarding address and phone
    number

3 Months–D-Day

Continue search
  Maintain contacts
  Revise and send résumés
  Telephone follow-up
  Schedule appointments
  Update and duplicate files
  Personnel dossier
  Medical and dental records
Complete
  Interviews
  Travel and lodging plans
  Vehicle repairs
  Farewell engagements
Outprocess
  Property inventory and transfers
  Medical appointments
  Personnel processing

D-Day and Beyond

Plan resettlement
  Housing
  Utilities
  Household goods delivery
Continue transition
  Update strategy
  Network
  Research
  Respond to ads
  Dispatch résumés
  Continue interviews
Savor success
  Evaluate job offers
  Negotiate
  Sign contract
  Begin new life
Follow up
  Acknowledge networkers
  Send thank-you letters
  Record lessons learned
  Assist other veterans

Neatly record the following entries:

Objective goals	Important appointments
Family plans	Coordination contacts
Scheduled interviews	Packing and moving schedule

The use of a large calendar permits you to easily see the increasing amount of time commitments and the associated coordination required. Color coding entries will be especially helpful. Protect your data from accidental spills by using permanent-type markers.

Daily Journal

This will be your diary for logging:

Items accomplished	Significant activities
Important names and places	Things to follow-up

Keep all your entries brief and concise. A short synopsis that can trigger your memory will be sufficient. Depending on the amount of detail that you desire and the size of your calendar, you can easily record this information on your planning calendar.

Whether you decide to use separate or integrated planning calendars and daily journals, both must be accurate. These documents will be convenient future reminders, especially during tax preparation time. Keeping a journal also provides you and the family with a small psychological boost because it is a concrete record that goals are being achieved.

Directory Log

You should keep a simple record of important names, addresses, and phone numbers. This can be your networking log too. Be careful of to write legibly; misaddressed letters waste time and mispronounced names are embarrassing.

COMPANY INFORMATION

Create a folder or notebook to contain your research notes on various companies. Keep all entries in a uniform format. Some critical data that should be included:

Firm's name, address, and phone number
Type of business (products or services offered)
Size of company (number of employees and sites)
Summary of research (your key interest items)
Important names (future contacts)
Interest items (useful interview questions)
Special notes (personal comments)

This consolidated information is very useful for comparing industries. It is also a handy source of information for developing your own interview questions.

Correspondence File

Use separate file folders for all your incoming and outgoing letters. Maintaining these files will help you keep track of responses to your résumés and applications. They are also an excellent resource for future re-contacting, network sharing, and job-hunting proof for your unemployment office counselor.

Interview Results

You should make a self-critique of each interview session. Some important points to record:

Your initial reactions (pros and cons)
Interesting questions that were asked
Answers that will require refining
Perceptions about the company (how you fit in)
Documents requested by the interviewer

Keep all your planners and diaries, even after your transition is completed. These documents will be helpful when it's time to make your next career move.

FINANCIAL RECORD KEEPING

Business Deductions

Tax laws change so frequently that it is difficult to predict accurately what Uncle Sam will impose next year. But here are some traditionally valid and legitimate suggestions:

Visit a reputable financial consultant *early* to map out your strategies for spending, saving, investing, and business planning.
Keep *all* your bills and receipts.
Record *all* business transactions.
Consult with a trusted accountant or tax preparer, preferably one who is experienced with military career changes.

The cost of contracting an employment search firm is deductible, but only if you are seeking a civilian occupation similar to that you had in the military. Here are some examples of valid and invalid deductions:

☐ **Valid.** A Coast Guard sonar operator searching for a similar position aboard a scientific research vessel; a GS-12 budget analyst looking for a corporate accounting position; a Marine embassy guard seeking a job in private security; a spouse working as a GS-6 secretary seeking a like position in private business.

☐ **Invalid.** An Air Force flight mechanic seeking a job as an arms merchant; a GM-14 personnel specialist searching for a commodities exchange job; a naval electronics engineer looking for a medical technologist position; a dependent employed as a GS-4 electrician's assistant seeking a new position as a restaurant manager.

Keep in mind tax law changes. Consult with a reputable accountant or knowledgeable tax preparer about recent changes in the tax law and the eligibility of any suggested deductions.

To effectively take advantage of your tax deductions, you must file an itemized return, and your expenses must exceed that year's standard deduction threshold. Keeping accurate and complete tax records will undoubtedly benefit you regardless of your eligibility.

Business Records

Determining your financial status will help you set monetary goals and spending limits. A set of concise records will also permit you to easily reference your available resources and to adjust your plans accordingly.

Press on if you already have a reliable system for recording and maintaining your business expenses. The following is for the few who may need a little bit of help. A simple and effective method is to maintain a journal. A typical student spiral notebook makes an excellent journal. There are many accounting techniques. Here are two examples to help you get started.

First is the *chronological journal*. Merely record each daily business expense incurred. Be sure to enter:

The date	Services received
Amount spent	Products purchased
Miles traveled	Business activities conducted

You may find it helpful to paste or tape your receipts directly into the journal. Avoid using new abbreviations with each entry; by tax preparation time, you may have forgotten what the abbreviations stood for.

This all-in-one concise log eliminates the need to keep several separate files. Later, you could review and categorize your entries, using the possible categories below.

Second is the *categorized journal*. Separate your log into specific sections. To minimize paper work and the need for later recalculations, use the Means Calculations form in Appendix A. You may also copy the format from IRS Form 2106, Employee Business Expenses. Here are some more categories:

Vehicle usage: gasoline, oil and maintenance, and miles driven

Local transportation: buses, trains, taxis, tolls, and parking fees

Distant travels: airline tickets, taxis, rental cars, road maps, dry cleaning costs, and lodging

Business: tuition, job training, word processor, business clothing, telephone bill, business-only credit cards, stationery products, office supplies, résumé reproduction, postage stamps, faxing costs, business cards, business club memberships, subscription fees for professional and trade journals, and tax preparation

Meals and entertainment: business lunches and social networking for employment opportunities

Charity gifts: clothing contributions to lighten your moving load or to make way for a new business wardrobe

Moving: unreimbursed storage and delivery expenses

A final suggestion concerning record keeping and taxes. Make sure you provide a reliable forwarding address for your final IRS W-2 Form. Otherwise, plan on writing your main finance and accounting center in early January of the year following your separation. Contact your local finance office for the center's address. If you do have to write, include a copy of your last wage record or leave and earnings statement (LES) to help expedite processing.

In addition to maintaining accurate financial records, you should also possess a readily available reference file.

REFERENCE FILE

The following suggestions will help you locate and prepare a list of advocates who will justly endorse your work performance and overall character.

Develop a ready list of several references, including superiors, subordinates, and peers. The more references the better; this permits you to rotate the names to different employers to prevent overuse. Remember, if the same people are continually contacted, they may lose their patience and interest in supporting you.

Famous celebrities or people with impressive titles are always appealing to employers. References need not be limited to those in your work environment. Consider other people who have observed your performance and are familiar with your abilities and reputation. Possible sources exist in your neighborhood, school, social club, athletic group, church, banks, and volunteer organization.

Be sure that the references you select are reliable, enthusiastic, and trustworthy people who will undoubtedly provide their objective opinions that you are the best person for the job. Request their permission to use their name as a reference and alert them to the possibility of frequent phone calls and letters.

Brief your reference people. Request your references to prepare themselves to respond to inquiries concerning the following characteristics:

Professional competence
Capacity to grasp concepts and acquire knowledge
Demonstrated expertise and competence
Display of sound judgment
Accuracy and thoroughness in performance
Commitment to excellence
Ability to work under stress
Positive enthusiasm
Ability to motivate and develop subordinates
Support for equal opportunity
Clear and concise oral communication
Clear and concise written communication
Adaptability to changes

Personal ethics
Dedication and commitment
Sense of responsibility
Integrity and honesty
Obedience to the law
Loyalty and devotion
Optimistic attitude

Moral standards
Selflessness
Candor and frankness

Special recognition
Participation in civic activities
Awards and commendations
Notable achievements

Inform your references of your job objectives and relevant qualifications. Provide them with a copy of your résumé so that they can speak "intelligently" about you when contacted by potential employers. Ask them when is the best time to receive telephone calls. Pass this information on to your interviewers.

Obtain formal Letters of Recommendations and References *before* you separate. These will come in very handy after you have separated and departed post or when all of your would-be references have been transferred to distant duty stations. Use some of the guidelines above to help you get started. Record their forwarding addresses and phone numbers for future reference.

Refer to Appendix D, Sample Dispatches, for a sample reference request letter.

In addition to references, make copies of your best efficiency reports and have them available upon request at interviews or to accompany job applications.

Locate the nearest fax machine; an employer may request immediate information. Also familiarize yourself with overnight mailing services.

Use your references judiciously. Employ your planning schedules as blueprints for constructing your future. Be flexible when necessary, but try to keep to your goals and plans. By examining your assets and liabilities, you can improve your investment of resources, especially your time and money.

To assist in the refinement of your plans, the next chapter will stimulate awareness of many of your hidden intentions.

INSIGHTS

Self-perception and understanding of your ambitions are key elements for plotting a successful future. By determining your own distinctive order of life's priorities, you can better develop a flexible series of successive objectives, each one leading you closer to achieving your ultimate goal.

This self-revelation should not be done in a vacuum. Involve your family in this momentous project. Individual aspirations must be united and merged with the intentions of other family members.

EVALUATING THE PAST

Consider yourself fortunate if you are in a military specialty with easily transferable skills. The demand remains high for most technically trained professionals. Only a minority will become outpaced by technology or necessity. Even those with extensive education and training must be continually invigorated with new knowledge and techniques to maintain their competitive edge.

If you are presently in a less marketable occupational specialty, seriously consider retraining into a more profitable profession. This viable option is particularly suitable for advance planners, especially those with the resources of time, aptitude, enthusiasm, patience, and money.

Another alternative is to transform an enjoyable avocation into a paying vocation. Many veterans have successfully turned a relaxing hobby into a prosperous career. Most become affluent, if not monetarily, at least intrinsically.

Those presently serving in a combat arms specialty already realize that their tactical expertise is not in high demand in the civilian world, at least not legally. Fortunately, defense contractors occasionally seek out tactical-type veterans to serve as technical advisors and consultants. But think carefully before pursuing a career in the defense industry. Even though this is one valid option in transitioning your military skills, defense contractors are notorious for unpredictable employment stability.

Combat-skilled veterans may also find hiring opportunities at some movie studios, military schools, news agencies, and think-tanks. Many Fortune 500 companies actively recruit new corporate soldiers to fill their management ranks. Ideal candidates are highly motivated, aggressive, goal oriented, and team players.

Although your military expertise, tactical skills, and wartime experiences may not be completely marketable, your leadership and management skills developed through the years are priceless. In this area, you have a marked advantage over those just graduating from school or in nonleadership positions. Even when compared with civilian colleagues who graduated with you from college or high school, you have a distinct advantage because you have had a greater diversity of social experiences. You have amassed much knowledge and experience in your unique travel adventures; exposure to diverse cultures and ideas; management of a wide variety of precious resources, equipment, and materials; responsibility for valuable properties and facilities; maintenance of sophisticated systems and components; and leadership and care of the most priceless commodity of all—people.

Despite the need for civilian retraining, you have supervisory and administrative credentials that are superior to those of most civilian job competitors. Highlight these skills in your résumés, cover letters, applications, and interviews. Employers are constantly seeking proven leaders and achievers.

That brief look at your past achievements should underscore the important accomplishments that will shape your future. Remember that the importance of experience is not necessarily where you have been but where it leads you. To better gauge your potential, you and your family should perform a realistic self-analysis of what you want to do for the next several years and where you want to do it.

CONTEMPLATING THE FUTURE

Draft a list of what makes you and your family truly joyful about yourselves and happy in life. Together decide what you would like your station in life to be 1 year, 5 years, and 10 years from now. Consider the following aspects.

Life-Style

Do you basically want to live like you do now? If you voted for a better life-style, then ask yourself, how much better? How do you mentally picture the future you and your future home?

Geographic Location

Where do you want to live and work? Where does your family want to live? What are the employment opportunities in those areas? During your military travels and relocations, you probably developed a preference for a specific part of the country, perhaps even a certain state or city.

Avoid limiting yourself to just one area because everything changes. The charming little community you used to lived in a couple of years ago may no longer be as you remembered it.

Evaluate your family's educational opportunities. If you have teenage children, consider where they want to attend college. Evaluate the future benefits of lower tuition costs for in-state residents.

Keep in mind your climatic concerns; cost of living; income tax structure; proximity to leisure activities; access to military exchanges, hospitals, special schools, or handicap facilities; and the demographic characteristics of the area.

For geographical information, do library research, write state tourism bureaus and local chambers of commerce, and contact old friends still living in your favorite places.

Employment

What work sector are you going to pursue—government, large corporation, smaller private company, family business, or self-employment? To focus your thinking, itemize all those aspects of work that you do well and that bring you the greatest satisfaction.

PRIORITIZING OBJECTIVES

Following are several lists of objectives to help you answer the above questions. Use these to identify your priorities and stimulate your thought process. Be sure your goals are consistent with your interests, values, and skills. Take plenty of time to carefully examine these lists. Rearrange them to meet your own order of merit. Add your own unique goals that are not shown.

Ideal life-style
Happy family life
Pleasant home and neighborhood
Close proximity to special facilities
Enjoyable and satisfying work
Self-employment
Owning a business and being the boss
Personal and business challenges
Safe working community
Steady advancement
Career security
Religious and spiritual fulfillment
Independently wealthy
Debt free
Customized home ownership
Luxurious physical comforts
Early retirement
Spontaneous vacation travels

Financial security for the family's future
Guaranteed old-age health care

Ideal company
Outstanding products and services
Nationally known and respected
Responsive to consumers' needs
Reputation for honesty and fairness
Legitimate and sound business management
High-technology or innovative approach
Competitive team spirit in the marketplace
Cooperative team spirit in the office
Genuine interest in your future
Advancement opportunities
Superiors responsive to personal problems
Safe operating conditions and practices
Tranquil working environment
Exciting operating conditions
Excellent social membership privileges
Long-term marketability of products
Close proximity to residence
Educational opportunities
Positive motivation and enthusiasm
Challenging and rewarding environment
Encourage suggestions for improvement
Active involvement in major decisions
Continual growth and company expansion
Nationwide and overseas offices
Advanced business practices
Efficient organizational structure
Excellent business location
Pleasant working environment
Use modern computers and machinery
Company physical fitness program
Casual dress codes

Ideal job
Challenging work
Clearly defined duties
Clearly defined authority

Being your own boss
Independent control
Assigned working staff
Availability of production resources
Flexible work schedules
Freedom for creativity
Enjoyable relationships with co-workers
Positive communications flow
Team-building opportunities
Excellent salary and benefits
Scheduled cost-of-living increases
High-performance bonuses
Timely promotions
Company car
Travel opporunities
Ability to work at home
Exposure to other job positions

By reorganizing these lists, you should gain a better understanding of the life-style and workplace that most interest you. Occasionally review these lists. In a few short weeks from now, you may be surprised to discover that your priorities may have changed.

Record these priorities and review them before a job interview. Knowing your priorities will be very useful when your interviewer asks, "What interests you about our company?" "What are you after in a job?" "Where do you picture yourself in a year, 5 years and 10 years from now?"

If you still need help in determining your new vocation, or narrowing down your desires, then a professional assessment may be appropriate. The Strong Campbell Interest Inventory that you completed in high school or college is available at most installation's education centers. Contact your education counselor for more information. Most schools and colleges also offer this free testing program.

The U.S. Department of Labor publishes two complementary reference books that are worth scrutinizing. Both are available at most libraries. *The Occupational Outlook Handbook*, which is issued annually, describes 250 vocational fields, highlighting their work environment, training qualifications, required skills, and salary ranges. This handbook is particularly useful for matching military experiences with civilian job-skill requirements. *The Dictionary of Occupational Titles* and its supplements offer a concise listing of hundreds of job titles and is convenient for translating some military titles into their civilian equivalents.

CHANGING TIMES

Consider the following interesting trends that are developing. Many people are changing careers more frequently. To keep pace with technological advancements and fluctuations in the marketplace, you, too, must be willing to continue to learn new skills.

Part-time employment and job sharing are growing increasingly popular as a way to schedule our busy lives to maximize self-efficiency and productivity. Also many people are continuing to work later in life, even beyond age 65. Some elect to work for the pure pleasure of working, while others continue to work out of absolute economic necessity.

Keep these new trends in mind. Remember that the more you learn and share, the more valuable you become to any employer, and especially to yourself.

One of the best investments you can make in your future is to learn another language. A sufficient working knowledge or fluency in one or two foreign languages will be an added bonus to your corporate credentials. Thousands of companies are expanding their markets overseas, especially in the European, middle Eastern, and Asian theaters. Opportunities also exist in foreign companies doing business within the United States.

As the walls of oppression are torn down, the competitive forces of free commercial enterprise are quick to invade. Think of the potential impact your knowledge of an appropriate second or third language can have on your future success. Enhance your proficiency by learning the proper conversational dialects, the subtle nuances of social and business customs.

Education is critical to everyone's success. While you are considering learning another language, also consider improving your computer literacy. Your knowledge and proficiency in the use and programming of modern computer systems will be an invaluable asset.

As you progress in life, you will find it useful to periodically evaluate your past performances and future desires. By reordering your old priorities in view of revised new ambitions, you can keep the winds of change from blowing you off your chartered and steady course.

To help you maximize your understanding of various career options, and to develop an unrestrictive search, the next chapter will describe some job opportunities with the federal government both at home and overseas.

CHAPTER 6

THE RETURN OF UNCLE SAM

Civil service is often a natural extension of a military career. Your public contribution continues, only now you are wearing a different uniform. Acceptance for mid- and senior-level government positions is becoming more competitive, however. With salaries and benefits closely approaching their civilian counterparts, government jobs are attracting more workers from the private sector. With today's economy, the popular notion of long-term job security is now part of a bygone era.

JOB SOURCES

There are several channels for locating available federal positions. I recommend using all options to maximize your list of possible job openings.

First, contact the local Federal Job Information Center; it should have a complete listing of all available openings in the region. Ask to review the current *Federal Job Opportunities List*. Centers located in major metropolitan areas usually provide self-service computer terminals to access federal job announcements.

Second, check your state employment office. It should receive copies of federal announcements for openings within your surrounding states. Beware that its listings may not be as complete or up to date.

Third, contact the specific federal agencies that you are interested in. Their local field offices may have advance knowledge of impending vacancies and future new positions.

A commercial publication entitled *Federal Career Opportunities* should also be reviewed. This booklet is published twice each month and is an outstanding consolidated listing of the majority of announced openings worldwide. Review it religiously on the 1st and 15th of each month because some announcements have very short application deadlines. This is where your precompleted SF-171 form (more about this later) will come in handy for quick mailing.

The booklet is available at some libraries. You may have to ask the reference librarian, however, because the current edition may not yet be shelved. You can also obtain a subscription by writing:

Federal Research Service, Inc.
P.O. Box 1059
Vienna, VA 22180-1059.

Federal Jobs Overseas

In Alaska, Hawaii, the U.S. Territories, and at U.S. installations in foreign countries, most vacancies are filled by locally eligible Americans, dependents, or foreign nationals. Therefore these openings are not publicized outside their local areas.

For information about these overseas opportunities, write to the Federal Job Information Center at the following addresses.

ATLANTIC REGION (PUERTO RICO, PANAMA, EUROPE):	PACIFIC REGION (ALASKA, HAWAII, U.S. TERRITORIES, ASIA):
Office of Personnel Management 1900 E Street, N.W. Washington, DC 20415	Honolulu Area Office Office of Personnel Management Federal Building, Room 1310 300 Ala Moana Boulevard Honolulu, HI 96850

SAUDI ARABIA:
Department of the Army
Saudi Arabia Consolidated Civilian Personnel Office
Riyadh, Saudi Arabia
APO New York 09038-5005

Keep in mind that overseas opportunities are extremely limited. The U.S. government prefers to employ qualified locally available Americans and foreign nationals. This contributes to the economy of that country and eliminates the expense of transfer travel costs and overseas cost-of-living allowance (COLA) pay.

There are many administrative, technical, and supervisory positions in which U.S. citizens are needed, however. Contact the Department of Defense (DOD) for opportunities. The DOD remains America's top employer of overseas personnel and is the agency with the most available vacancies.

Employment opportunities also exist with many other federal agencies, including the Foreign Agriculture Service, DOD Dependents Schools, National Oceanic and Atmospheric Administration, the State Department, the U.S. Information Agency, the Army Corps of Engineers, the Agency for International Development, and the Peace Corps.

Other Government Opportunities

The federal employment maze is astonishing. As a veteran, you already realize the incredible amount of bureaucratic red tape that must be cut through. Expand your options and research possible municipal, county, and state government positions.

If you are a retiring regular commissioned or warrant officer, you will benefit by obtaining a nonfederal government job because your retirement pay will not be affected. The Dual Compensation Act of 1964 requires the reduction in these officers' retirement pay if they begin to draw a federal paycheck. The still-current 1988 formula requires a reduction of one-half of your annual retirement pay in excess of $7,698.41. Fortunately enlisted personnel and reserve officers are exempt from this law.

Maximize your opportunities by applying for several civil service positions at various government levels. Beware, however, that just as in the military, government agencies are subject to mandatory force reductions, hiring freezes, limited hiring, and slow promotions.

THE APPLICATION PROCEDURE

Once you have located a prospective opening, check the announcement to make sure that you meet all the requirements. Pay particular attention to education, experience, skills, and abilities. If you are satisfied that you are competitively eligible, make application for the position.

Apply as early as possible, especially for a federal job. Applications for some positions take several months to process. The waiting time depends on the number of applicants, how many eligible people are already waiting, your standing on the merit list after completing the necessary tests and interviews, the time it takes to complete background investigations, and the ever-present budget constraints, temporary hiring freezes, permanent cancellation of job announcements, and office politics.

The majority of federal applications are processed through the regional Office of Personnel Management (OPM). Some major federal agencies, such as the U.S. Postal Service and the Central Intelligence Agency, are exempt from OPM hiring practices and have their own application forms and selection procedures.

If you are interested in specific federal agencies, contact their field offices or Washington headquarters for appropriate application procedures. Addresses and phone numbers are in your local telephone directory's Blue Pages or can be obtained by calling your friendly reference librarian. If you are told that an SF-171 is required, then read on.

The SF-171 Form

To start the procedure, you must first complete an Application for Federal Employment (SF-171) form. These forms are readily available at any local OPM office. Also check your post or base personnel office and federal field offices. Obtain several copies in case you make a mistake.

While requesting the SF-171 form, also ask for the pamphlet *Veterans' Preference in Federal Employment.* This booklet contains general information about determining a veteran's status, preference in examination, credit for time served, and retirement pay restrictions.

Thoroughly and accurately complete the SF-171 form. *A detailed listing of your accomplishments in the description blocks will greatly benefit you in receiving a higher merit rating from the examiner.*

You will have to complete a separate SF-171 form (copies are acceptable) for each federal position you are applying for. Therefore, leave blank on your original SF-171 and SF-171-A (continuation sheet) forms:

Block 1 (job title) on SF-171

Blocks 48 and 49 (signature and date) on SF-171

Blocks 3 and 4 (job title and date, again) on SF-171-A

After reproducing sufficient copies, you may then complete these blocks for each separate application.

Preferences for Veterans

If a written federal test is required for a specific position, your rating will be based on your performance. Many veterans are eligible for additional credit (5 or 10 points) to be added to their test scores. Here are a few guidelines on veteran preferences.

Retired regular commissioned officers (0–4 and above) are not eligible for preferences unless disabled or retired from the active reserves.

Five points will be added if you:

Entered on active duty between October 15, 1976, and September 7, 1980 (reservist: October 15, 1976, and October 13, 1982), *and* received a campaign badge or expeditionary medal;

Enlisted after September 7, 1980, or entered active duty on or after October 14, 1981, *and* completed 24 months of continuous

active duty, *and* received or are entitled to receive a campaign badge or expeditionary medal;
Are a disabled veteran.

Ten points will be added if you:

Were awarded the Purple Heart;
Were disabled but not eligible for compensation;
Were disabled (less than 30 percent) and eligible for compensation;
Were disabled (30 percent or more) and eligible for compensation;
Are a spouse, widower, or mother of a deceased or disabled veteran.

Recent veterans of the Persian Gulf war should also check with the appropriate hiring agency for additional new preference points.

Vacancies for mid-level and senior-level (GS-9 through GS-15) are not filled through specific examination. If no test is required, your rating will be based on your education and experience, which is listed by you on the SF-171 form.

Filing Period

The government will accept applications only for specified filing periods, announced positions, pay grades, and locations. They will not keep your SF-171 form on file for future openings; you must reapply each time an announcement is made of a particular position.

You may still file an application after the filing deadline, provided the vacancy has not been filled and you were discharged within 120 days of the filing deadline. Contact the applicable hiring agency to determine if you have "delayed filing privileges."

Notice of Eligibility

After mailing in your application(s) and taking any required tests, expect to wait up to four months before receiving a Notice of Results that indicates your eligibility. If you are eligible, your name will be placed on a merit list with other candidates and the list will be forwarded to the actual agency with the opening. They will, in turn, review your application and standing on the merit list. Subsequently, you will be informed if there is any interest in offering you the job. But there are some exceptions.

Occasionally federal agencies have authority to directly hire eligible applicants without regard to their standing on the merit list. This applies to occupations (teachers, secretaries, clerks, and typists) that have a shortage of highly qualified applicants. Some positions (watchmen, janitors, and messengers) may not require any eligibility notice.

For positions GS-9 and above, order of merit lists may not be maintained. Only a final notification letter will be received after the selection is completed.

The elapsed time between applying and finally hearing from Uncle Sam can be very long. And what you finally hear may not please you. It is not uncommon to receive a response letter nine months after you submitted your application.

If you are accepted, then expect another wait until your name reaches the top of the waiting list. You may also have to wait for a school date. Your patience should be rewarded.

Or perhaps you would rather try for something in the world of business. More about that in Chapter 7.

IT'S A CORPORATE WORLD

Welcome to the novel life of business suits, power ties, portfolios, and *The Wall Street Journal*, the world of car pools, stale office air, desk life, computer stations, ringing telephones, fluorescent humming, yellow stick-em notes, water coolers, office politics, three-martini lunches, Alka-Seltzer, and rush-hour congestion.

A job is opening up in some company, somewhere in our world every minute of the business day. A position becomes available when an employee resigns; is fired, promoted, or transferred; or becomes disabled, retires, or dies. Opportunities are also created when companies expand or change locations. On the flip side, executive jobs are reduced or eliminated by mergers, reorganizations, acquisitions, trade market downturns, and major economic recessions.

THE MILITARY EDGE

Fortunately many companies do actively recruit veterans. They know that service people bring with them into the workplace a variety of tangible and intangible skills and talents. Veterans are experienced professionals who are:

Highly motivated, dependable, and disciplined

Technically trained, with many transferable skills

Committed team players striving towards excellence

Strong leaders who quickly adapt to crisis situations and capable of working under pressure

Mature people who are able to set priorities

Responsible and possessive of a strong work ethic

Remember these fine qualities. They are important facts to broadcast in your cover letters and interviews.

The length of time it takes to secure employment is influenced by some of the following:

Your intended profession

How saturated the market is with your specialty

Where the company is located

The present economy and future economic outlook

Your personal qualifications

Competition from other perspective employees

How you appeal to the interviewers

The present mood of the prospective employer

Your standing on the waiting or merit list

Public demand for your services

Even the season of the year

Disregard the old myth that you cannot be offered a job during the summer. Despite summer vacations, college interns, and relaxed attitudes, many veterans are hired between Memorial Day and Labor Day. Also the festive period between Thanksgiving and Valentine's Day is another open season. The opportunities may be less during these periods, but your success in filling a job vacancy will directly depend on your own efforts.

ESSENTIAL READING

This is where you begin your research and study in earnest. After careful reading of many dozens of how-to books on changing careers, marketing yourself, résumé writing, and job searches, I discovered several outstanding books that will be of tremendous help to you.

You are strongly encouraged to read these books. All will improve your insight and provide you with very useful hints. These books are listed in a sequential order to best help you develop your foundation of knowledge.

☐ *Super Job Search: The Complete Manual for Job-Seekers and Career-Changers*, by Peter K. Studner (Los Angeles: Jamenair, Ltd., 1989) is a superbly complete all-source guidebook. Read this one first.

☐ *The Professional Job Search Program: How to Market Yourself*, by Burton E. Lipman (New York: John Wiley & Sons, 1985) is written in a humorous and conversational style. It describes various interviewing techniques that you can anticipate and provides sample letters and résumés.

☐ *The Résumé Catalog: 100 Damn Good Examples*, by Yana Parker (Berkeley, Calif.: Ten Speed Press, 1988) is an outstanding collection of sample résumés arranged in 12 broad job categories and covering 160 occupational titles.

☐ *Throw Away Your Resume & Get That Job*, by Warren J. Rosaluk (New York: Prentice-Hall, 1983) gives excellent suggestions for preparing for interviews, including questions to ask, and tells how to negotiate salary.

☐ *The Job Belt: The Fifty Best Places in America for High Quality Employment Today & in the Future*, by Joseph and Amy Lombardo (New York: Penguin Books, 1986) provides an excellent demographic overview with listings of major employers.

☐ *International Jobs*, by Eric Kocher (Reading, Mass.: Addison-Wesley, 1990) is an excellent source for developing your foreign connections and learning how to contact overseas employers.

☐ *Where to Start Career Planning 1989–91: Essential Resource Guide for Career Planning and Jobs*, edited by Carolyn Lindquist and Pamela Feodoroff (Princeton, N.J.: Peterson's Guides, 1989) is a super resource, listing hundreds of available publications on different career fields and employment topics.

☐ *Peterson's Job Opportunities for Business and Liberal Arts Graduates* (Princeton, N.J.: Peterson's Guides, 1991) and *Peterson's Job Opportunities for Engineer, Science and Computer Graduates* (Princeton, N.J.: Peterson's Guides, 1990) provide excellent cross-indexes of industries and starting locations. The guides also match academic background with employment opportunities, give company addresses, descriptions, and points of contact.

This list is by no means all inclusive. Undoubtedly there are many other fine books on the market. These were selected for their practicality, ease of understanding and application, and overall usefulness. Obviously you may not be able to obtain all of these books, therefore some were selected because they provided the same basic information.

You are encouraged to read other books, especially if they pertain to a profession you are seriously considering. Be careful not to flood yourself with information overload. Try to read just one book a day so that you can properly digest the knowledge.

These books are very popular and should be available at your base or local public library. If your library does not have copies, ask your librarian to get a loan from another library. Expect to wait anywhere from several days to several weeks, depending on where they obtain the loaner. Save yourself some time and check out the mall's bookstores. Several are worth owning. Pause now to collect and read these books.

EMPLOYMENT OUTSIDE THE UNITED STATES

Just as there are government jobs overseas, there are corporate jobs overseas. In addition to the experience of living in another land and culture, overseas jobs offer some tax advantages. Most civilians working in non-U.S.-government jobs overseas are exempt from U.S. taxation of all or part of their foreign wages. To qualify, you must be a bona fide foreign resident for an uninterrupted full tax year, or for 330 days during any period of 12 consecutive months.

Once you have established foreign residency, your voting by absentee ballot in any U.S. election will not jeopardize your foreign residency status. Temporary vactions or business trips back to the United States will not terminate your status.

As of now, you can exclude up to $70,000 of your foreign-source earned income, prorated by the number of days in the year that your tax home was abroad. Tax laws are constantly changing, however. Telephone an IRS representative to verify current residency requirements and exclusion amounts.

After completing your reading assignment, you should be ready to draft your first résumé. Remember this will be your trial attempt. It is almost guaranteed that you will need to make several revisions. The average is usually five tries before you develop a résumé that best presents your marketable talents.

You will discover that as your résumé improves in content quality and appearance so, too, will the number of favorable response letters and invitations to interviews. It takes as much effort to send out poor résumés and letters of introduction as it does to send out great ones, so from the outset plan to send only the best.

The best résumés are the one that get you invited to interviews and land you job offers. As you develop your résumés, always remember that the universal business motive of all companies is Making Money! You must now refocus your endeavors to support that objective.

Drafting your first résumé can be a daunting chore. By following some simple step-by-step guidelines, you can change this task into another challenge. I will tell you how in Chapter 8.

YOUR RÉSUMÉ

Just like the military, most companies have their own infrastructure, take care of their own, and promote from within their ranks. This is a reality of life that you must acknowledge. Fortunately, as you learned earlier, companies do look outside the company to fill some positions. You must seize these limited opportunities to advertise yourself.

All too often jobs are not offered to those who are best qualified. Instead they are offered to those who best promote themselves and their skills.

You may never again attain a civilian position with the same authority and responsibility that you possessed in the service. Therefore, you must carefully review your *entire* life and draw out all those hidden talents and skills that make you unique. You must package these qualities and sell yourself to your next employer.

SELLING YOURSELF

Prepare now to take a giant leap forward and begin the intricate process of merchandising your valuable talents.

☐   **Step 1.**   Prepare photocopies of all your efficiency reports (Officer Evaluation Report, Senior Enlisted Efficiency Report, Fitness Report) and academic evaluations. If your service uses Evaluation Support Forms, those will also be very useful. Make only one-sided copies of each document. You will be highlighting, cutting and pasting, and marking on each sheet. The quality of reproduction is unimportant—just so it is legible to you. Never write on your originals, you may need them later.

☐   **Step 2.**   Identify all your significant duties and responsibilities. Use a highlighter to mark the beginning of each sentence. Be sure to indicate your specific duty titles. On a separate sheet of paper, include:

Other major duties and responsibilities

Secondary and alternate duties

Specialized duties and skills

All informal requirements not officially recorded (do not reveal any classified information)

Add to this list all responsibilities acquired "out-of-uniform" before, during, and after your service tour:

Part-time jobs

Summer employment

Free-lance projects

Community service activities

Volunteer work (avoid listing anything that may be controversial in nature)

Club memberships (professional, civic, social, athletic, church, and recreational)

☐   **Step 3.**   Review your lists of duties and cross out any redundant or similar statements.

☐   **Step 4.**   Identify all your significant accomplishments. Use the same technique as above but use a different colored highlighter to avoid later confusion. Include any recognition, education, or training you received, such as:

On-the-job training
Awards and commendations
Vocational training
Correspondence courses
Computer proficiency
Knowledge of government contracts and regulations
Special programs

Repeat the process listing all unrecorded and civilian accomplishments:

College courses
Scholastic honors
Personal and professional licenses
Publications and presentations
Training certificates
Foreign language proficiency
Extracurricular awards
Community achievements
Volunteer work
Meaningful personal victories
Overcoming physical or learning disabilities

This expanding list should include specific examples of the *positive results* you have achieved:

Management of materials and resources
Development of projects and products
Supervisory leadership of people
Participation in major decisions
Conservation of resources
Reduction in expenditures
Improvement in quality
Increase in production

Special recognition

Management in crises

Tip: Another excellent summary of your achievements can be found in the narrative citation on your award certificates.

☐ **Step 5.** Review your lists of accomplishments and cross out any redundant or similar statements.

☐ **Step 6.** Translate statements of duties to actual specific achievements. For example:

Responsibility: (A) Directed training of 40 people.

Accomplishments:

(A-1) Developed and implemented a 21-week training program resulting in the award of the Annual Base Commander's Excellence in Training Trophy.

(A-2) Designed a reusable training device that saved the base $5,500 a year and was adopted for use throughout the service, increasing the potential savings to $2.3 million.

You may find it easier to cut out block statements of related accomplishments and arrange them together under the appropriate heading of Responsibility. Then paste your combined duties/achievements onto a separate sheet of paper.

If you find cutting and pasting too tedious, consider giving a code to like duties and achievements. For example, assign the letter A to a specific responsibility and write that letter next to the highlighted statement. Then locate all associated achievements and simply write A-1 next to the first accomplishment, A-2 next to the second, and so forth.

☐ **Step 7.** Continue this process until you have exhausted your lists. Expand your lists of achievements by writing powerful "one-liners." Combine action verbs with specific results (see examples in Appendix C, "Action Words and Phrases"). Draft sentences that vividly connect your effectiveness, efficiency, and responsibility with improving production, enhancing quality, and streamlining procedures.

You now have the skeleton of your résumé. Place the project aside for a day to clear your mind.

□ **Step 8.** Now its time to "demilitarized" your résumé. Your military achievements must be translated into language that any civilian can understand. Avoid the use of military terms and jargon in your résumé unless, of course, you are sending a résumé to a military contractor; they may understand your military terminology.

The translation process will initially be difficult. You are rightly proud of your military history and want to advertise your achievements. But, remember, your new audience will be civilians.

Most will not understand the significance of your military duties; some may have a predisposed bias; and some may even be turned off. Be proud of your military service and do not camouflage your record, but do translate your various military skills into understandable civilian business terms. Always tailor your presentation to the audience you will be addressing.

To help you get started, the following is a partial list of some suggested civilian job titles that often are applicable to the military ranks shown. Because of the diversity of classification systems in use and size of companies, these "officer equivalents" are only examples of one plausible hierarchical order:

GENERAL AND FLAGSHIP
OFFICERS
President
Senior director
Chairman of the board
Special military consultant

SENIOR FIELD GRADE OFFICERS
(05,06)
Chief executive officer (CEO)
Chief operating officer (COO)
Chief financial officer (CFO)
Senior vice-president
Executive vice-president
Chief executive
Defense contracting advisor

FIELD GRADE OFFICERS (04)
Senior administrator
Chief executive
Department head
Program director
Deputy chief
Senior executive

COMPANY GRADE OFFICERS
(01–03)
Executive
Manager
Associate
Deputy assistant
Superintendent
Operations officer
Administrative officer

SENIOR NCOs (E7–E9)
Director
First supervisor
Department manager
Section chief
Coordinator
Representative

WARRANT OFFICERS (WO1–WO4)
Director
Specialist
Technician
Facilitator

People in many technical occupations are bonded through the use of job-unique lexicons. If you are in one of the following vocations and are planning to move into a parallel civilian career, you may find it beneficial to continue using your own job title and terminology:

Accountant
Analyst
Architect
Carpenter
Chef
Electrician
Engineer
Firefighter
Investigator
Journalist
Lawyer
Mechanic

Nurse
Pharmacist
Photographer
Physician
Pilot
Plumber
Police Officer
Scientist
Teacher
Technician
Translator
Programmer

Be careful not to over- or underrate your qualification title. Some companies have their own unique hierarchy; for example, some firms simply refer to all employees as associates. You may have to contact each of your prospective companies to determine their preferred ranking methods.

WORD PROCESSING

You are right if you have figured out that a word processor would come in handy right about now. If you own a computer with word-processing capability, you are strongly encouraged to use it. If there is one at work, ask your boss if you can use it during nonpeak hours (lunchtime and before and after work). For obvious reasons of liability it is not recommended that you take home any expensive or sensitive equipment.

You may have to take some quick lessons on how to operate the computer. Remember to record the system's model number because you can now add this new achievement to your résumé under the category of Computer Proficiency.

If you use the computer at work or borrow one from a friend, be sure that you will have access to it throughout your search. This includes the time following your separation, when you have moved off post. Otherwise you will end up with a disk full of information and no compatible computer on which to use it—another good reason for buying your own.

If you are concerned about the big price tag, think of it as a major investment in your future. Besides, you can always sell it later, after you have gotten your new job. And if you decide to keep it for use in your work, you can claim it as a business expense and deduct a portion of its cost from your taxes.

A VALUABLE SUPPORT SERVICE

You are encouraged to read *Marketing Yourself for a Second Career*, an excellent booklet full of fruitful information and some good samples of "civilianized" résumés. The booklet costs $3 and is available from:

The Retired Officers Association (TROA)
201 North Washington Street
Alexandria, VA 22314-2529
Tel: (703) 549-2311

The booklet is also available for free at the free lectures that TROA gives dealing with the same topic. Call your Public Information or Public Affairs Officer for the date and place of their next lecture.

TROA additionally offers a program called TOPS, the TROA's Officer Placement Service. Entry into this system requires membership, which costs $20 a year. Besides receiving a monthly magazine and copies of job referral notices, other benefits include résumé preparation assistance, career counseling, and access to TROA's Career Research Center. These services may be very useful to those living or visiting the Virginia area.

RÉSUMÉ FORMATS

Through your reading you will have discovered that there are dozens of résumé formats, writing styles, and philosophies about which is best. The three most popular formats are: chronological, functional, and performance.

Chronological Format

A traditional and time-honored approach, the chronological format lists your jobs in reverse order. The directors of most corporate human resources divisions (the new designation for the old personnel departments) are used to seeing this format.

Begin by listing each of your job titles separately, starting with your present one and working backward. Remember to "civilianize" your military title. For example, crew chief may be translated to team supervisor, commanding officer to managing officer, and so forth.

For each duty position that you list, include specific:

☐ **Employment dates.**   Use either the month and year or year alone.

☐ **Locations.**   Names of obscure military installations are usually meaningless to most employers. I recommend your using a familiar city, state, or country.

☐ **Specific duties.**   Carefully link your important responsibilities with significant achievements. Describe your role in the unit, number of people you supervised, special equipment you operated or managed.

Repeat this process for each previous job.

Functional Format

A reliable and effective format, the functional résumé highlights by categories your marketable and uniquely *applicable* skills and knowledge for a specific job.

The functional categories should relate directly to and support your explicitly stated career objective. The following is a partial list of some popular specialities that you may have performed or managed:

Administration	Marketing
Aviation	Medical
Budgeting	Operations
Communications	Personnel
Computers	Planning
Construction	Procurement
Contracts	Promotions
Development	Public relations
Efficiency	Quality control
Finances	Research
Logistics	Security
Management	Training

Within each functional area, briefly describe your accomplishments without breaking them down by separate job titles.

Performance Format

An excellent blend of the best features from each of the above, the performance résumé combines a functional style with a chronological format.

This unique format provides sufficient flexibility for creativity and tailoring the content to specific job objectives. But exercise extra caution if you select this technique. Avoid the possible hazard of not focusing your talents to support a specific job objective. Only you can decide which style is most comfortable for you and best presents your valuable talents.

Making a Choice

To determine which format best advertises your skills and potentials, refer to the following recommended guidelines.

Use the chronological format when you:

Are making a move into a similar civilian career field (for example, medical, legal, engineering, transportation, and aviation);

Have served the majority of your professional life in one primary occupational specialty and want to illustrate a positive pattern of development and achievement;

Have other unique, transferable skills requiring little retraining.

Employ the functional style when you:

Are making a dramatic career shift (for example, from infantry to social work);

Have served in various different occupational positions and have limited specialized or concentrated work experience;

Want to emphasize specific experiences by focusing on skills relevant to your new occupation.

Utilize the performance technique when you have:

Open-ended career goals;

Training in a variety of specialities and desire to merchandise a total picture of your potentials;

Varied experience that is best highlighted and supported using this combination technique.

Pause for a few minutes and turn to Appendix B, Sample Résumés. The illustrated sample résumés show the progression and dramatic difference that a few revisions of the same information can make. Quickly scan the various résumés and then return to learn more helpful hints.

If you are a fairly good writer, experiment with different formats. There are no restrictions on what is proper and correct except on that rare occasion when a company has a required résumé format. You will eventually develop your own unique style and winning form.

No matter what format you select or personally design, be sure to include the following elements.

Primary items
Personal data
Objective(s)
Highlights of qualifications
Professional experience
Education and training

Secondary items
Performance summary
Unique accomplishments
Work history
Future potential
Special qualifications
Honors, awards, and achievements
Foreign language proficiency
Associations and affiliations
Presentations and publications

Ask several friends and colleagues to critique your résumé for spelling errors, grammar, style, accuracy, and completeness. If you need help in the writing department, consult a knowledgeable friend or family member.

For professional help, try a résumé-writing service. Warning: many may not be able to successfully translate your military duties and experiences into civilian terms. Shop around for a service that offers quality, military expertise, and reasonable production costs. Remember, *you* are your own best promoter.

DOS AND DON'TS

Here are some résumé dos and don'ts and other pertinent recommendations based on hard experience.

☐ Always make a positive first impression. Your résumé is your first presentation to a prospective employer. What the executive or personnel manager initially sees and reads will make the difference between an interview offer, a rejection letter, or immediate circular filing. Your résumé will allow a prospective employer to evaluate your ability to express yourself concisely in an organized and coherent manner.

☐ Be serious in your job search. Do not send out résumés just to go through the motions. You are wasting the company's time and, more importantly, you are wasting your own precious time.

☐ Be creative in your presentation if you want to capture a prospective employer's attention. Imaginative résumés may be most effective with advertising and public relations agencies and marketing firms. You need your résumé to stand out from the hundreds of other competing résumés but not to be so different that you are misinterpreted as a complete oddball. Always think about your audience. A splashy presentation to a conservative organization may not be effective.

☐ Avoid all military jargon, acronyms, and abbreviations unless you are applying for a government or defense contractor's job, in which case the recipient will undoubtedly understand your lingo. Translate all technical terms into relevant and and identifiable civilian skills. Have your résumés reviewed by an outsider who can spot your military terminology. You may have becomed desensitized to your routine environment, particularly your use of work-related language.

☐ Highlight your accomplishments with specific results. Do not list your responsibilities without accompanying achievements. Employers want to know what your jobs were and, more crucially, how well you did them.

☐ Quantify with numbers your appropriate achievements. For example: decreases in required work hours; increases in production quality, personnel trained, budgets managed, resources conserved, and expenses saved.

☐ Use actual numbers: $250,000 has a greater visual impact than *two hundred fifty thousand dollars.*

☐ Emphasize the diversity of your special accomplishments, especially if you lack the desired levels of formal education. Accentuate the importance of transferable on-the-job training as another valid substitute.

☐ Personalize each résumé by presenting only the relevant information that a specific employer may be interested in. For example, highlight your investigative skills if you are applying for an researcher's job. Downplay or eliminate irrelevant skills such as managing the post's championship basketball team—unless, of course, you are applying for a researcher's position with an athletic team or sports company.

☐ Keep your complete résumé *under two pages*. Anything longer may risk the possibility of being ignored or misinterpreted as an example of your inability to be brief, clear, and concise.

☐ Dispatch only high quality reproductions of your résumés. Do not send carbon copies to save money; it will be interpreted as unprofessional for an executive business environment. Invest the money for professionally reproduced copies, but limit the quantity. Printing fees are expensive, especially for changes, and you will definitely be making changes. Test market a small batch first. A word processor will certainly enhance your ability to individually tailor each résumé.

☐ Provide an accurate address and phone number(s) where you may be contacted. Seriously consider buying an answering machine, especially if no one is home during the day. An answering machine is especially useful for recording calls from across the country; remember the differences in time zones. If you are a constant traveler, consider call-forwarding telephone service. Test your answering machine frequently to avoid missing important calls.

☐ Avoid including names of references on your résumé; just state that references are available upon request. Review the suggestions offered in Chapter 4, "For the Record."

☐ Train your office workers and children to understand the importance of phone calls from prospective employers. Instruct them to be courteous and to record all messages accurately and completely. Instruct them not to comment, even favorably, on your personality or work habits; the caller may misinterpret the conversation. Remind your children about keeping the telephone line open during business hours.

☐ Locate the nearest fax machine in case an employer requests immediate information. Familiarize yourself with overnight mailing services.

☐ Anticipate numerous "no replies" and rejection letters. This is your gauge of résumé effectiveness. Letters acknowledging receipt of your résumé may take up to one month to arrive. Also, some companies may not have the money to respond to all inquiries. Rejection and "under consideration" letters may take two or three months.

☐ Some companies may wait until the final application cutoff date before beginning the résumé screening process. The earlier you send in your résumé, the longer you may have to wait. But always dispatch your résumés as early as possible; this is to your advantage if the company evaluates résumés on a first-come, first-answered basis.

☐ Rejections are inevitable. Do not become depressed. The more résumés you send out, the more nos you will receive, but also the more opportunities to receive yeses. And one true yes is all you may need.

☐ Save all of your rejection and "Your qualifications are being reviewed to determine if their is presently any suitable match . . . but we will retain your résumé in our active files for six months should a suitable position becomes available . . ." letters. Most of these responses are from actual decision makers. You now have an excellent list of names to recontact at a later time or to use for networking with other interested parties or sharing with friends.

☐ Always send an accompanying cover letter with your résumé. Do not send any résumés without some form of introduction to let the prospective employer know what your objectives are.

☐ Keep your résumé up to date, even after you have successfully completed your transition. By keeping it fresh, you can prevent yourself from having to reinvent your own career wheel. Your résumé remains an excellent quick-reference to your past and future.

Stop here and turn back to Appendix B. This time make a detailed examination of the sample résumés. Extract all those essential ingredients that you can use to make your own personalized résumé an impressive success.

Once you have completed a draft of your first résumé, put it aside for a few days. You will be surprised at how time can sharpen your self-marketing acumen and writing style. It also makes detecting errors much easier.

While your résumé remains temporarily dormant in a closed desk drawer, continue reading on. Just as you should never send a young child out at night alone, never send your résumé out into the cold world alone. Jacket it with an introductory cover letter.

YOUR COVER LETTER

The cover letter is your premiere performance to the company. In essence it is a written sales proposal marketing your own valuable skills. By showing that you can successfully advertise and sell yourself, you hope to convince the prospective employer that you can do the same for the company's products and services.

Your cover letter is a personal introduction to your past experience and future potential. The cover letter and résumé constitute a personal "credentials package" that you are sending to a prospective employer. While your résumé selectively defines your marketable talents, your cover letter stimulates the reader to want to read your résumé.

SENDING A MESSAGE

The appearance and content of your letter will produce an equivalent mental image of you. An intelligently written letter that is neat, organized, brief, concise, and focused will reflect positively on you.

Creating an initial favorable impression will substantially improve your chances of being offered an interview.

Your letter should be special, yet remain within the limits of acceptable business practice. As you receive correspondence from various corporations, you will see that most adhere to essentially the same standard format. (Turn to Appendix D, "Sample Dispatches," to see several illustrated suggestions.)

By personalizing each letter, you will demonstrate your diligent research efforts and writing skill. Begin by addressing each letter to a specific influential person in the company. Occasionally insert the company's name into the body of the letter.

Locating the right decision maker is often difficult in a large and complex organization. In Chapter 10 you will discover how to uncover some of those key action people.

If you are applying for an entry level or nonprofessional position, you could start with the company's employment department. For mid- and senior-level management and professional positions, you will have better success by contacting senior management officials.

Starting at the top and letting your request trickle down the chain of command may not always be effective. It may be interpreted by some as bucking the system; by others, as bold initiative. Use your discretion.

THE CONTENT

The basic components of the body of your cover letter will vary, depending on the type of letter you are sending. Most self-sell letters should contain, as a minimum, the following essential paragraphs:

Introduction	Résumé preface
Background synopsis	Follow-up contact
Integrated match	Appreciation

☐ **Introduction.**   Remember the last time you started to read an article or watch a movie. If in the first few moments your interest wasn't captured, you probably flipped the page or changed the channel. This same standard will be applied to your cover letter. Your letter must stand out from the thousands that an employer may receive. Your introductory paragraph must intrigue and subtly compel the reader to continue reading.

Tailor your presentation to your anticipated reading audience. Carefully research each company or vocation by using some of the information sources that will be provided in Chapter 10, "Networking." You will learn that trade publications, local periodicals, and the firm's advertisements and annual reports are all excellent sources of useful information.

Identify and ascertain any significant trends, recent developments, or problem areas that you can specifically mention in your introductory paragraph. You can attract attention by complimenting the company on a specific achievement, including the name of an important company person, or commenting about a unique new product the company is developing.

Exercise caution when using words of praise. They could send a wrong signal, making your letter sound bogus, conceited, or pretentious (apple-polishing). Besure that your flattery is genuine, sincere, and properly directed.

To use name-dropping effectively, you must actually know someone in the firm. Or you can resort to some imaginative tactics, such as telephoning a key company official and discussing some related current affair. This permits you to legitimately use that person's name as an initial contact source. Because the reader will be unaware of your actual relationship, to be safe, he or she will likely assume that the relationship could be a relatively close one.

Identify your job objective within or after your introductory paragraph. Examine the manner in which you present your employment pursuit. Unless you are applying for any available position, or a specific position, be careful not to be too general or too restrictive. For example:

"I am requesting employment for a career management position within Paragon Industries."

"I am seeking an operations management position with responsibilities for overseas functions."

"I am soliciting consideration for a senior-level executive position with overall responsibilities for overseas operations."

☐ **Background synopsis.** Briefly highlight your talents that are *directly relevant* to the position you are seeking. You can accentuate the relevancy with examples from your education, training, or experience, but abstain from just repeating information that is already included in your resume.

☐ **Integrated match.** In this paragraph, you should further exploit the information you have acquired about the company. Emphasize how your distinctive talents can successfully be used to fulfill the firm's particular needs (for example, how you can help solve a particular problem). One technique is to "template" the match between the company's advertised requirements and your compatible skills.

☐ **Résumé preface.** Move smoothly into inviting the reader to further explore your exceptional abilities by reviewing your résumé.

☐ **Follow-up contact.** Explain that you will establish future contact by phone or in person. Request an interview to personally amplify your assorted abilities to enhance the company's sales, image, future.

☐ **Appreciation.** Graciously thank the reader for this opportunity to present yourself. Your courtesy will be remembered as another reflection of your personality and professionalism.

With experience you will be able to successfully mix, match, and blend combinations of prepared narratives. If you are investigating several career options, research each vocation, then dispatch similar cover letters and résumés to those firms within that vocation. As you narrow your selections, personalize each letter and résumé for a specific company, job, or person.

SOME SAGE ADVICE

The content of your cover letter will be limited only by your imagination. To improve your success rate, here are some fundamental lessons learned:

Limit your cover letter to one page.

Address it, by name, to a specific person whenever possible; recheck spelling of names.

Never address it "To whom it may concern."

Include the title of the addressee.

Keep comments brief.

Always use positive, upbeat statements.

Convey an honest and enthusiastic tone.

Never overexaggerate your experience.

Use an attention-grabbing introduction.

Commend the company for its reputation or a recent achievement (for example, winning a contract), if applicable.

Identify your job objective.

Highlight a few of your relevant achievements.

Do not duplicate information that is on your resume.

Describe how the company can effectively exploit your unique talents.

Introduce your résumé.

Explain how and when you will make follow-up contact, or invite them to contact you.

Express your appreciation for their interest.

Avoid explaining long unemployment gaps, lack of specific education or experience.

Refrain from mentioning your salary requirements (unless your letter is to a placement firm).

Always double-check spelling, punctuation, grammar, brevity, style, and format.

Turn to Appendix D and closely scrutinize the following sample cover letters for various occasions:

Request for a letter of reference

Generic cover letter to a company

Letter responding to job announcement

Thank-you letter after an interview

Letter to a recruiting firm

By now you may have some great ideas to include in your own cover letters. If you need more ideas, review *The Perfect Cover Letter*, by Richard H. Beatty (New York: John Wiley & Sons, 1989).

Remember that while your résumé will illustrate your ability to organize information, your cover letter will convey your personality, creativity, and writing ability.

If you are still experiencing "temporary technical difficulties," a short break may be fitting to relax and clear your thoughts. When you are ready, you will be guided to your next journey stop—how and where to discover job information.

CHAPTER 10

NETWORKING

PROBING THE MARKET

Locating the names and addresses of companies with job openings is an exciting challenge, especially for those with a bit of Sherlock Holmes in them. As you may have noted in your reading, statistics vary about the best places to locate job openings. Here is an overall approximation of the findings: 60 percent, networking; 15 percent, employment search agencies; 13 percent, advertisements in periodicals; and 12 percent, letter campaigns.

Tapping the Network

Everybody belongs to a network—that delicate information web of family, friends, and colleagues, any one of whom is a potential source of insider's news about impending job vacancies. As you trace your intricate pattern of contacts, you will find that one source often leads to another.

More than likely you, too, will find your next job through a trusted old friend, probably one who recently separated from the service.

85

It's time to locate those old business cards and address books. Establishing a network with old and new veterans may prove rewarding on both a professional and personal level. You can also learn from their mistakes and share new information.

Seriously consider pooling your resources with other separating members who have your same interests and goals. You may reap a substantial savings in time and money, develop valuable business associates, and promote long-lasting friends.

Your networking success depends on your ability to:

Accept the fact that you need other people's help

Let everyone know that you are job searching

Actively seek out new leads

Ask for advice and not a job

Present a well-rehearsed positive description of your employment goals

Clearly identify your intentions to employers

Convincingly promote your skills and potentialities

Conscientiously follow through with contacts

Continue the process until successfully completed

When you contact associates and friends, instead of asking for a job, request their guidance. This avoids placing them in an awkward position and removes any hesitation they may have in helping you. By seeking their advice, you are also subtly complimenting them.

Remember mitosis and cell division from high school biology? Similarly, your networking assets will multiply in a complex chain reaction.

Recognize the needs of your spouse. If you are planning a major geographical trek, your mate may also be job hunting. Use teamwork; combine your resources and expand your networking exposure.

Be inventive in searching out networking contacts. You may have to resort to some uncoventional intelligence-gathering techniques. Consider the potential usefulness in establishing a good rapport with the following information assets: bankers, investors, receptionists, secretaries, vendors, customers, competitors, delivery people, printers, newspaper writers, realtors, clean-up crews, barbers, waitresses, and shoeshine people.

Trade unions are another source of contacts. Local chapters of national unions are listed in the Yellow Pages. Union members are a superb source of advice and networking.

You should also visit professional trade shows to learn the newest developments for your intended profession and to make valuable contacts. Admission is often free or reasonably priced.

The Hidden Job Market

To successfully penetrate this underground network, once again you must rely on your ingenuity and initiative. Combining the assets listed above with your network of family and friends should provide an excellent starting base for job opportunities.

Knowing the right people is only a part of the solution, however. Your sources must also know and trust you. Confidence must be earned and built upon. To obtain accurate and timely job leads, you must subtly inform your network of what special signs to look for:

Bank approvals of new business loans
Media announcement of contract awards
Increased activity in the "office grapevine"
Scheduled opening of new branch offices
News releases of employee promotions and transfers
Orders for more supplies to new job sites
Newly printed advertisements not yet released
News stories of business expansion
Plans for new construction or renovation projects
Discarded confidential memos
Announcements posted on company bulletin boards
Casual conversations gleaned from service workers
Interoffice computer messages of future openings

Most of the above activities are positive indicators of increased business. With increased business comes the corresponding potential for new employment opportunities. Any newspaper leads that sound interesting and promising should be further investigated. Be sure to collaborate with other sources to substantiate accuracy. Remember that your response must be quick because the window of opportunity will probably be very limited.

Contact the company for more information. By establishing yourself as a "known quantity," you increase both your exposure and the likelihood of an invitation to interview. This initiative and interest may also be remembered commendably by potential employers.

Employment Search Agencies

These headhunters advertise in various newspapers, magazines and phone directories. Look in the back of any *Army Times*, *Navy Times*, *Air Force Times*, or *Federal Times* and you will see several listed.

Some agencies have search and placement services that span the nation, but most concentrate on a specific geographical area, usually limited to the contiguous states. Some restrict their services to specific specialties, such as nursing or aerospace engineering. There are four basic varieties of employment search firms.

☐   **Firms that act for client companies.**   Large corporations often engage these search firms to locate prospective new employees who have specific skills and experience. If the firm is successful in locating such a candidate and the company ultimately hires that person, then the company will pay the search firm a finder's fee, usually a certain percentage of the first year's salary.

In essence, these search firms exist to satisfy the needs of their client companies and not the needs of the job seeker. Therefore, if you send them your résumé, do not expect to hear too much from them unless your skills match the requirements of the client company. Remember, the recruiter's loyalties are with the company.

Rest assured that if a company has any interest in you; the search firm will contact you because you are their "bread and butter." You would be smart to contact these types of search firms. There is no direct cost to you and such contacts expand your opportunity network. But be careful; some companies may try to negotiate a lower first-year salary to reduce the cost paid to the search firm.

☐   **Firms that act for the job seeker.**   You contract with and pay these firms when they are successful in placing you in a company. The fee may be a set amount or a percentage of your first year's salary. This may appear to be a relatively risk-free option, but exercise caution.

Even though the fee is not paid until after they locate you a job and you are actually hired, there are no guarantees of how long you will remain employed. If you quit or get fired after a few weeks, the fee paid the search firm may not balance in your favor. Never pay any money in advance; you have no guarantee that the search firm will even be in business tomorrow.

☐   **Firms that act for either company or job seeker.**   Some search firms are combinations of the above two types. Either the client company or the job seeker may be responsible for paying the placement fee—sometimes both. Always shop around and compare prices.

☐   **Firms that offer multiple services.**   These agencies may advertise themselves under a variety of grand-sounding "professional" and "executive" banners. Many are legitimate operations providing fine, reputable, and honest services. Some are deceptive swindlers defrauding thousands of honest job seekers.

Caveat Emptor

A legal disclaimer: reference to any actual agencies, or any similarity between persons, places, or events in this fictional scenario is purely coincidental and unintentional.

For about $5,000, these multi-service marketing agencies promise to provide psychological testing; career counseling; personal résumé preparation and mailing; access to updated job announcements, computerized job searches, international periodicals, secretarial support, office space, 24-hour answering and paging services, and more. Does this sound too good to be true? You are probably right. Be extremely cautious of appealing ads offering lucrative salaries, high-level job titles, advanced placement, instant access to the job market, computerized targeting of companies, and guaranteed rapid employment.

There are probably many fine, descent, and honest firms that do provide such reputable services. Unfortunately, there are also many charlatans with impressive titles, splendid offices, and prestigious addresses, all waiting to exploit the emotionally vulnerable, depressed, and desperate job seeker.

If you unwittingly answer one of their deceptive ads, expect to receive a phone call from a secretary urgently summoning you to an important interview. Because you have already sent out dozens of résumés, you may be confused about who this is; after all, it might be a job offer. So you respond and find yourself in one of these offices. Now stay alert for certain warning signs.

While seated in the waiting area, the secretary may begin your indoctrination by boasting about the firm's successes. You look around the nicely furnished office and notice a name board congratulating newly employed members of the program. You may even see the familiar Better Business Bureau membership emblem, visual confirmation of the firm's authenticity and integrity. Finally you are greeted by the interviewer.

The "Doctor" (or other impressively titled character) may begin by presenting to you, on paper, a synopsis of his career, an exquisite portrait of his years of helping people just like you. It may also contain a few accolades to his academic achievements, valuable contributions to the community, and membership in the church.

He—or it could be a she—starts the conversation by telling a few war stories because he, too, is a veteran. Having departed from the service a few years ago, he sympathizes with what your are experiencing. He may applaud your accomplishments and assure you that a person with your skills should be worth top dollar.

An offer is then made to help find you a job with a 20 percent salary increase. He next casually and shrewdly asks what your present salary is. He may also nonchalantly inquire about separation pay, cashing in your leave, and other earnings. Watch carefully; this is when he begins taking cryptic notes, calculating how much he can take you for.

The discussion continues with a description of the firm's excellent network of high-level contacts in many companies and assurances that getting you that right job will be no problem. Once he thinks you have swallowed the bait, he may then spring his next trap.

He says how much he admires your initiative in wanting to start the program immediately so that you can be behind your new desk in a few short weeks. He then shows you a blank contract to let you see that there is no fine print or anything to hide.

At this point you may be offered a contract at "substantial savings" if you make a lump-sum payment. He may even graciously include a "serviceman's discount" just for you.

If you sign the contract and pay the fee, several months later you will have a handful of résumés, received some "psychological counseling," spent hours reviewing old information, be thousands of dollars poorer, and probably still have no job.

Be extra careful as separation day approaches, especially when your employment prospect looks gloomy and emotional spirits are low. This is your window of vulnerability, when you become an easy target. In desperation you may unwittingly visit one of these deceptive firms. They may even contact you, using their own network of informants or by enticing you through phony job ads.

Thoroughly research any employment, placement, or counseling firm. Talk to your friends and associates who may have used their services. Contact the Better Business Bureau (BBB) for any record of complaints.

Keep in mind that the BBB is not a government agency. It does not investigate, give legal advice or credit information, pass judgment on services, ask for refunds, arbitrate (decide who is right), or enforce any contracts. The BBB is only an advocate for fair business practices and a promoter of consumer confidence. It does provide general consumer information and frequently serves as a mediator (go-between). Membership in the BBB does not constitute legitimacy or guarantee ethical practices, it just indicates that a company has paid a membership fee to join.

Before doing business with any agency, request a randomly selected list of past and present customers. If the agency is legitimate, this should not be a problem. They will be correct if they say that they must protect the privacy of their clients and cannot give out phone numbers. In that case you should ask the agency to get permission from those individuals so that either you may contact them or have them contact you. Be suspicious of preprinted lists of "satisfied customers." Some may be coconspirators in their ruse.

Before you sign any contract or pay any money, always demand a *complete* contract and then go over it with a reputable lawyer. Examine the contract for unusual fees, refund policy, penalty payments, nullifying conditions, and inclusion of an "escape clause" if you decide later to cancel their services.

Avoid becoming another victim of a multimillion-dollars-a-year fraud industry. Remember this scenario and save yourself thousands of dollars and much grief. End of lecture and now back to realty.

Advertisements in Periodicals

☐ **Newspapers.** Do not downplay the significance of newspaper job advertisements. They are an excellent source for expanding your network. Carefully read the announcements. The companies usually state their specific requirements. Use this information to prepare your cover letter and résumé by highlighting the "unique match" between your talents and their needs.

Be wary of ads without a company name or with only a forwarding address. It is not uncommon for blind ads to be placed by headhunting firms trying to expand their resource pool by compiling a list of active and qualified job seekers. These ads may also be placed by tricksters, as illustrated above. Some companies may even run false ads as a loyalty test to detect who in their own company is secretly seeking to get out.

Blind ads are also used by genuine companies wishing to confidentially protect their interest. Official job announcements may influence the stock market, alter their competitors' strategy, create rumors, cause internal dissension, or embarrass those destined to be terminated or reassigned.

When in doubt about the legitimacy of any blind ad, you could apply this simple technique. Send a letter requesting more details. Your letter can be anonymous, signed with a pseudonym or sent by a third party.

Large city newspapers are excellent sources of currently advertised regional and nationwide job openings. Sunday editions are especially useful. Many companies prefer to advertise their major and multi-available positions on Sundays, because these journals often have the highest readership and the largest national circulation.

Keep your eyes open for jobs fair announcements, which are also usually published in Sunday editions. Larger libraries generally carry the majority of these journals. Subscription addresses are listed in Appendix E.

The National Ad Search, a weekly journal containing hundreds of job ads compiled and reproduced from 74 major U.S. newspapers,

including some of those below; ads categorized into more than 50
careers ranging from accountant to zoologist

The National Business Employment Weekly, a collection of regional
ads appearing in *The Wall Street Journal*

The Atlanta Journal and Constitution

Chicago Tribune

The Los Angeles Times

The New York Times

The San Francisco Examiner & Chronicle

The Washington Post

☐ **Trade journals.**   These periodicals contain ads soliciting specialized skills. If these journals are unavailable at your local library,
try visiting a local office where the "trade" is being practiced. For
example, visit your eye doctor for optometry periodicals, or a major
hotel for hospitality magazines.

☐ **Association journals.**   These professional publications are excellent sources for learning a trade's vocabulary. They also carry ads
listing job openings. Schedule a visit to a major university library;
most carry a large variety of specialized periodicals.

A catalog of published trade magazines and association journals can
be found in *Where The Jobs Are: A Comprehensive Directory of 1200
Journals Listing Career Opportunities*, by S. Norman Feingold and
Glenda Ann Hansard-Winkler (Garrett Park, Md.: Garrett Park Press,
1989).

Letter Campaigns

Launch a letter-writing campaign to ferret out job opportunities. To
bolster your efforts, I have listed some very useful references below.
Once again, this is not an all-inclusive inventory; only the ones that
were found to be the most productive and readily available are included. You may discover some very good sources in your own journey. The majority of these publications should be available at any
well-stocked library.

The following are annual publications containing the names and
addresses of leading American and international corporations. They
also identify the names of chief executive officers.

The Career Guide: Dun's Employment Opportunities, published by Dun's Marketing Service.

Million Dollar Directory, published by Dun & Bradstreet.

Standard & Poor's Register of Corporations, Directors and Executives, published by Standard & Poor's Corporation.

Always check the year of publication. It would be embarrassing to address a letter to someone who departed the company a year ago, especially if that person had been fired.

Some other resources include:

☐ **Phone directories.** These are always a reliable source of addresses and telephone numbers. Most public libraries carry many major metropolitan phone books. Some libraries also possess a microfiche version of *all* directories nationwide.

Ask your librarian for the following specialized telephone directories. They provide categorized listings by trade and geographical states. Most major companies also have a toll-free 800 number, giving you a free means of contacting the companies for actual names to which to address your résumés.

AT&T Toll-Free 800 Consumer Directory

Business to Business—A Commercial/Industrial Buying Guide, by Bell Atlantic

Yellow Pages Nationwide Edition

Most advertisements in phone directories provide only the company's street address and not the ZIP code. Therefore, you will need the U.S. Postal Service's *National Five-Digit ZIP Code & Post Office Directory*, which is readily available at most libraries and all post offices.

☐ **Business magazines.** These periodicals contain hundreds of corporate addresses. Celebrated magazines such as *Forbes* and *Fortune* cater to major league corporations. Closely examine their articles and advertisements for addresses—a good place to start your search.

Each year both magazines publish in their April/May issues a list of their top-rated "500" companies. These issues provide superior and current intelligence data that you can use to compare prospective employers and to exploit for future interviews.

Write to the companies you are interested in and request a copy of their current annual report to the stockholders. These excellent and comprehensive reports highlight a company's business status, profits and losses, recent developments, and future projections. They also include the names (some with photographs) of key executives whom you may consider contacting.

☐ **Consumer magazines.** Business weeklies such as *Money* and *Business Week* contain prepaid postcards for ordering free copies of annual reports. Remember to also request the companies' product brochures. These reports, along with the information contained in the magazine articles, are invaluable resources for preparing for interviews. You can subtly impress your interviewer by asking pertinent questions gleaned from the report.

ORGANIZATIONAL NETWORKS

Established military and civilian organizations are an invaluable resource for the job seeker.

The Military Connection

Several military associations provide job counseling, referral and placement assistance, and job fairs. Most provide these services as part of their membership package. Check out the following:

Air Force Association
1501 Lee Highway
Arlington, VA 22209
Tel: (703) 247-5842; (800) 727-3337 (ext 5842)

Association of the United States Army
Career Assistance Service
2425 Wilson Boulevard
Arlington, VA 22201-3385
Tel: (703) 841-4300; (800) 336-4570

National Association for Uniformed Services
5535 Hempstead Way
Springfield, VA 22151-4094
Tel: (703) 750-1342; Fax: (703) 354-4380

Navy League of the United States
2300 Wilson Boulevard
Arlington, VA 22201
Tel: (703) 526-1775

The Non-Commissioned Officers Association
225 North Washington Street
Alexandria, VA 22314
Tel: (703) 549-0311

Marine Corps Association
P.O. Box 1775
Quantico, VA 22134
Tel: (703) 640-6161; (800) 336-0291

The Retired Officers Association
The Officers Placement Service
201 North Washington Street
Alexandria, VA 22314-2529
Tel: (703) 549-2311

Other excellent referral sources are your local: Veteran Assistance Center, veteran organizations, the veteran employment representatives at the state employment office, and the Federal Job Information Center.

Civilian Contacts

The number of civilian referral, networking, and group counseling clubs is increasing throughout the country. Some are even available on your personal computer, via a network of electronic bulletin boards. Look in the current issue of *The National Business Employment Weekly* for the address of the nearest clubs. Most are free for the joining; the only membership requirement is that you are an active job seeker.

If you are 40 years old or older, consider contacting the Forty Plus

Club, a popular national organization that may be able to help you organize your search. Check your phone directory for the nearest chapter; most are in major cities. For more information, write:

Forty Plus Club of New York, Inc.
15 Park Row Avenue
New York, NY 10038
Tel: (212) 233-6086

This is a self-help type of club. Its local chapters are excellent sources for making new contacts and exchanging information. Because it caters to a more mature clientele who share a common age denominator, it can offer valuable exposure to past and present senior executives. Some chapters may even permit those approaching 40, or at least those with a few gray hairs, to join.

MENTAL BREAK TIME

You were in isolation. At the operations brief, you received a situation report, the latest intelligence, and were given a link-up mission and the necessary resources. You developed a plan of action employing meticulous search techniques. Target company-sized objectives were identified where you can employ your tradecraft.

Reconnaissance located a window of opportunity, a vacant position. You developed the situation using your surveillance network. A potential contact agent is sighted. An encoded communique is drafted using personalized one-time pads. Your signal is bursted to the asset; transmission is received and code broken. The source acknowledges your message. You're invited to establish formal contact via a live-drop interview.

Suddenly appearing out of the darkness is Karl Malden. He steps up to you and asks, "What will you do? What will you do to prepare for the first encounter. . . ?"

THE INTERVIEW

EVERYBODY'S NIGHTMARE

On "Face the Nation," a prominent invited guest faces a panel of seasoned interviewers. After a cordial exchange of repartee, the inquisition begins. The initial series of questions are easily answered; the guest appears relaxed and secure. Body language reflects his feelings: the legs are crossed; an ankle is slowly rotated counterclockwise; the jacket is unbuttoned; an elbow is propped atop an armrest; clasped hands are unfolded; gestures complement his delivery; he smiles.

Suddenly, in quick succession, a barrage of questions are fired from different panelists. More time is needed to formulate an intelligent response, but there is no time; the questions are piling up. Simultaneously, the guest answers one question, thinks about the second, while listening to the third.

The intense stage lights cause the guest to perspire profusely. He now reorients his body: legs are uncrossed and both feet are firmly planted on the floor; he sits erect, moving slightly forward to the chair's edge; hands are at the defensive ready position on the hips; the forehead wrinkles, pupils dilate, and the smile disappears.

The adrenaline-pumped guest is poised for action—the old flight or fight syndrome. He quickly scans the room for a rescue party; none is in sight. He thinks of escape but realizes he is trapped by the predatory panelists. Bizarre thoughts of public humiliation, family disgrace, unemployment, and his shoeless hungry children never going to Annapolis flash through his mind. Through the blinding glare he sees peace at last—a jump master, I mean a floor manager, signalling "one minute!"

He quickly adapts to the hard-line questioning technique. Now he is a seasoned veteran, ready to field the toughest questions. But too late. It is time for a commercial. . . .

Was that the twisted tale of an imaginary interview by a frustrated writer? Yes. A bit of exaggeration to point up the need for proper preparation, confidence, and control of body language.

PLANNING AND PREPARATION

An interview takes you one step closer to employment. This is probably the most challenging and rewarding phase of your transition. Interviews may be viewed in three parts: before, during, and after. Just as in any military operation, careful planning and preparation lead to smooth execution during the operation and result in a successful mission accomplishment.

Your life experiences have already demonstrated the importance of a good interview. Remember the many junior NCOs and officers you welcomed into your unit? How you quickly sized up their past, present, and even their future?

From the first knock on the door you made judgments about their personality, style, and work ethic. You examined how they carried themselves in their uniform, its crispness, their haircut and shave, the types and number of ribbons and decorations on their blouses, the spit and polish of their shoes, the pride in their salute, the exactness in their reporting procedures, the firmness in their handshake, how they sat, if they were prepared to take notes, how they answered questions, the knowledge they already possessed about your organization, the quality of questions they asked and, finally, how they departed your presence.

With that brief exposure to a weary, traveled, red-eyed, family-waiting-in-the-car, living-out-of-suitcases newcomer, you decided his or her destiny. You had the power to accept or reject them from your unit. All future encounters with them will now be colored by your first impressions.

As you sit at your first post-service interview, you realize that you are now on the "other side of the table." You are no longer in authority. But with careful preparation, you can still be in control.

An interview is your opportunity to demonstrate your self-assurance by behaving in a positive, courteous, and professional manner. Your spoken words and nonverbal cues will provide clues to your intentions, interests, and potentials. By words and demeanor you must communicate that you will not be a company liability, but a valuable asset with a valid contribution to offer and the credentials to support it.

Before the Interview

To supplement the information you have picked up from your readings, I offer some further suggestions to prepare yourself for the interview phase.

Thoroughly research the library for general information about the company. Ask the company to send you a copy of its annual report. Check for recent articles written about the company in business and trade magazines. For local companies, check local magazines and newspaper business sections. Do not rely on memory. Take notes about topics you may want to ask at the interview. This will demonstrate your seriousness and interest.

Expand your research from an individual company to an entire business sector. For example, if you are preparing to interview with IBM, do not limit yourself to learning about what is happening at IBM. Go one step further and learn about a trade competitor, such as Xerox or Wang. You can impress the interviewer by working in a comment or question about the top competitors. This really shows you did your homework. Remember that your investigation does not have to be exhaustive. Just find some general information to demonstrate your initiative and sincerity.

Send your wrinkled business suits to the dry cleaners. Save your best suit for the actual interview, especially if you have to travel a great distance. Polish your shoes and check the back heels for excessive wear; they are the last thing an interviewer notices as you depart the office.

Dressing for Success

Dress conservatively and be well groomed. If you are a woman, do not use excessive makeup. Do carry a briefcase or portfolio. Changing from battle dress uniforms to business suits is a wardrobe challenge. If you have not been in recent contact with the civilian corporate world and are unsure of what today's successful business executives are wearing, check the photographs contained in business magazines, as well as in *Esquire* or *Vogue*. Beware of short-lived and outrageous fads. Examine the dress of the people in the company's promotional brochures and annual reports. You may also do some undercover work.

Simply post yourself outside a large company at lunchtime. You should be able to quickly separate the short-sleeved white-shirted mail-room clerks from the tailored three-piece chief executives—and all those in between. Of course, this reconnaissance only works when the weather is nice.

During inclement weather, you may have to sneak behind the lines and check out the company's cafeteria, or nearby restaurants and taverns. You could also shadow some executives to their after-work hangouts. But be careful; they could misconstrue your actions as a hostile threat, in more ways than one. Hangouts are excellent one-stop locations for doing some networking, self-advertising, and intelligence gathering.

As you gradually develop and expand your civilian wardrobe, avoid transient fads. Remember Nehru jackets, leisure suits, psychedelic wide ties, and bell-bottoms?

Despite changing fashion trends, geographic locations, and seasons of the year, certain conservative outfits appear to always be in business style.

Men should choose traditionally styled dark suits in various shades of navy blue or gray, either pin-striped or solid. Natural wool fabrics generally drape the body better than synthetics. Basic light-colored shirts are best, with white still a time-honored favorite. Traditional ties come in paisleys, stripes, or plaids. Bright red ties command attention and are currently associated with power, but be careful not to overshadow your interviewer with a too-intimidating tie. Socks should also be subdued to avoid attracting unfavorable attention. Shoes should be black, brown, or cordovan, with wingtips a popular choice for decades. Carry a leather business portfolio or briefcase. Basic rings and watches are acceptable, but definitely no earrings or outlandish eyeglasses.

Women should choose a contemporary-styled two-piece suit or dress, in seasonal colors, with navy blue a year-round business favorite. Fabric selection depends on the outfit and the weather. Whether you select skirts or slacks depends on you; but be prepared, some companies still have specific dress codes. Light pastel-colored blouses or complementing tops are always in good taste. Contrasting scarfs and belts add color. Hosiery should be in shades of brown or gray. Fashionable basic pumps continue to remain in vogue, along with conservative heel heights. Carry a business portfolio or briefcase. Jewelry and accessories should be conservative and modestly worn.

The following books will provide more helpful hints about attire:

Dress for Excellence, by Lois Fenton (New York: Rawson Associates, 1986).

Dress for Success, by John T. Molloy (New York: Warner Books, 1984).

Look Like a Winner! by Lee H. Cass and Karen E. Anderson (New York: G.P. Putnam's Sons, 1985).

What to Expect

Be mentally prepared to be exposed to a variety of interviewing situations: formal, informal, individual, and by panel boards. Other interviewing techniques include:

☐ **Series interview.** You will meet with several interviewers, either individually or by departments.

☐ **Group performance.** This involves your active participation with other candidates or company members in solving an assigned task. Your contributions will be closely monitored and graded.

☐ **High-stress interview.** This is a staged performance to evaluate your tolerance and reactions.

☐ **Luncheon.** This approach efficiently utilizes the busy executive's time, allows him to write it off as a business expense, and lets him see how well you interact socially.

☐ **Candidates party.** You will be invited to a social affair at which a group of senior executives will evaluate and compare you with other candidates.

☐ **Telephone interview.** This method is used by many companies to screen a large pool of potential candidates for follow-up personal interviews. This technique is gaining popularity because it saves time and travel expenses. Prepare yourself mentally and vocally. Have your reference material ready for instant access.

Anticipate meeting some interviewers who are aggressive, prejudiced, one-sided, stressful, inattentive, and unprepared. Equally, expect to meet well-prepared top-notch professional interviewers.

The four most popular questions that interviewers ask are:

1. "Tell me about yourself."
2. "Why are you leaving the service?"
3. "Why do you want to work for us?"
4. "What are your best strengths?"

Now that you know the questions, be sure you develop brief, well-organized, and articulate responses. *Rehearse, rehearse, and rehearse.* Always practice your answers. Ask your spouse or best friend to critique you. Better yet, ask an acquaintance; you will probably receive more objective commentaries from near strangers. Use a videorecorder or simply practice in front of a large mirror.

Do not try to answer these questions cold; your unreadiness, combined with nervousness, will equal disaster. Refer to Appendix F, Typical Interview Questions and Responses, for some sample queries and answers.

Keep your responses relevant and to the point. Do not waste precious time by telling unrelated war stories, confessing your sins, complaining about your hardships, venting your anger at old bosses, or explaining your past. By composing a positive summary of your applicable achievements and specific qualifications, you can avoid falling prey to your emotions, or deviating from the questions.

THE BIG DAY

Be on time for all interviews. You may arrive early, but avoid arriving too early. This may indicate that you are too anxious or too frantic, and you may be in the way of others. Do arrive in sufficient time to review the company's annual report, provided you have called ahead and reserved it. Also, this is your prime time to size up any competition.

Freshen up in the washroom before the interview. Check yourself over from head to toe. You may find it handy to carry a small bottle of eye drops to "get the red out" and look your business best. Remember to have your handkerchief, reading glasses, and some breath mints handy.

Be kind and courteous to the receptionist and secretary. Do not ask them questions about office politics or the interviewer. Remember that the secretary is the boss's eyes and ears. What you say or do in the waiting area may be reported back to the interviewer.

Thoroughly and accurately complete all application forms requested before the interview. It is imperative that all forms be completed neatly, with a professional businesslike appearance. This is an important indication of your sincerity regarding the job. If the secretary hands you an extremely long application while you are waiting for the interview, ask if you may return it later. If she insists that it be completed now, politely explain that you would like more time to thoroughly complete the forms.

Do not complete the section marked "salary requirements." If you give a figure that is too low, the interviewer may interpret this to mean that you are desperate or that something is wrong. Give a figure that is too high, and you may place yourself outside the acceptable salary range for that job. Your salary request could be a discriminating factor that would remove you from further consideration. It is usually best to write in "negotiable depending on the job requirements." This is another good excuse for them to invite you to another interview.

Finally, keep your spouse and children away from the interview site. Do not let unnecessary distractions ruin your golden opportunity.

During the Interview

Remember my short story about the importance of first impressions. Apply all lesson learned from both the story scenario and personal experience.

Practice the three cardinal rules for all interviews:

1. Listen more and speak less.
2. Answer only what has been asked.
3. Never speak negatively about old bosses or jobs.

Start with a firm handshake and gracious greeting. Take the initiative for setting the tone of the meeting by making a sincere and positive comment about how pleased you are to be there.

Do not sit down until either invited to do so or after the interviewer is seated. The interviewer may play mind games to test your reactions by seating you across the room, on a broken chair, or in a shallow beanbag. You should remain calm and politely ask to sit closer or on another chair.

Project a sincere appearance of enthusiasm and confidence. Some recommend that you sit near the chair's edge and lean slightly forward to demonstrate your total interest. Others recommend that you sit squarely to show self-assurance. The correct answer is probably to sit in the posture that lets you feel most comfortable—within the bounds of office etiquette, of course. Try this practical style: sit squarely in the chair and, when a truly interesting question comes along, show sincere interest with a small natural lean.

Do not smoke, unless you are interviewing with a tobacco company.

Listen carefully to all questions. Some interviewers may have some fun with you by mumbling their questions and watching your reaction. Tactfully ask them to speak up. Be careful, the murmuring may be a genuine speech impediment. If you are unsure, listen awhile before you decide and act.

Think before answering. You may be given some rapid-fire questions to determine your reaction. Remember the "Face the Nation" example. Do not let the pressure show; control your emotions and remain confident. If you are well prepared, no question is a barrier. Do not hesitate to ask for a few seconds to collect your thoughts before responding.

Always be honest. If you do not know an answer, just say that you do not have an appropriate response now but that you will gladly furnish it later in a letter or phone call. Remember that the interviewer has probably asked the same questions dozens of times, and he will surely recognize any double-talk or bluffing responses.

Keep your answers brief and concise. Do not ramble. Talk less and listen more is a golden rule for interviews. Do accentuate the positive and elaborate on those areas in which you have strong expertise.

Maintain good eye-to-eye contact and be attentive. Do not embarrass yourself by asking a question that has already been answered.

Remain loyal to your former superiors, subordinates, and associates. Do not say anything negative about your old company or colleagues. Often questions may lead to how well you liked your bosses or co-workers. As difficult as it may be to speak kindly of some, always point out their positive aspects. The loyalty you display to them will be viewed as a reflection of your future loyalty to the company.

Take notes, but only if you absolutely must. Taking notes has different effects on people. Some interpret it as a sure sign of interest; others, as an discourteous distraction during a conversation. When in doubt, simply request the interviewer's permission to take notes.

Be professional at all times. Never try to argue with the interviewer. Remember who has the power over your destiny. If you are faced with an extremely antagonistic or prejudiced interviewer, avoid any confrontations by politely excusing yourself. Is surrendering your dignity worth any job?

Remain in total self-control. Emphasize all your unique attributes that positively establish your potential value to the company. Show how your abilities fill their needs.

Ask insightful questions. Have a list of questions ready. Some interviewers measure your interest by the quality and quantity of questions you ask. It will be impressive to pull out a short list of concise questions.

Do not ask about salary at this meeting. Wait until they display a hiring interest and make you a tentative offer.

If questioned about your salary goals, attempt to avoid any discussion involving actual figures. Some interviewers may query you on this topic to determine if your interest is purely monetary, or whether you are sincerely interested in being a company team member. Because you will not know their true motive, say that salary is just one factor in your consideration of any job offer.

Keep track of the time, but avoid appearing too obvious when you look at your watch. This may suggest that you are too impatient or are anxious to get out of there. Use other polite methods of timekeeping: casually glance at a desk or wall clock; look at the interviewer's watch,—when he's not watching, of course; or attach a small watch to your notebook.

Unless requested to spend more time, avoid overstaying your allotted interview time. Definitely do not overstay your welcome.

Ask what is the next step in the selection process and when you can expect to hear from them again.

Conclude the interview by summarizing your skills and telling how they will benefit the company. Very briefly, in less than a minute, highlight your unique abilities to handle people, information, and things.

Express your appreciation for their time, interest and hospitality.

Finally, declare that you want the job. After hearing their pitch, you may be undecided about whether you want to work for this particular firm. After careful thought, you can always decline any actual job offer later.

After the Interview

Perform a self-critique of your interview performance immediately. This will help you mentally close out this interview and prepare you for others.

Record your thoughts and feelings about your own reactions, responses, and rapport. Write down your strong selling points and those that will need refining. List any interesting questions that were asked so that you can develop improved answers for your next interview.

Chronicle your initial perceptions about the company, its corporate culture, formalities, and your impressions of the interviewer as a reflection of that company. Imagine how you will fit into that environment. Ask yourself how well you think the company meets your standards of acceptability.

Immediately forward all interviewer-requested replies and correspondence (for example, transcripts and letters of reference). Send a thank-you letter of card to the interviewer. Express your appreciation for the interview opportunity, briefly present any vital information not mentioned at the interview, restate your job-specific qualifications, and emphasize your enthusiastic interest in the job. For an example, see Appendix D, Sample Dispatches.

Extend your gratitude to all those networking agents who may have arranged your initial contact and interview favor.

Recontact the interviewers if you have not heard from them at the specified time, or in about two weeks.

With each additional interview, you will gradually develop greater self-confidence, project a more polished image, provide improved responses, refine your oratory skills, and perfect your presentation techniques.

Eventually you will successfully pass this recognition stage and enter the acceptance stage. Upon receiving several job offers, you will then be in the fortunate position of selecting your destiny. As you evaluate each proposal, compare all the relevant features with your list of prioritized ideals that you created in Chapter 5.

A major condition of each job offer will be your salary and additional perks. Chapter 12 will reveal what special benefits you can bargain for.

SALARY AND COMPENSATION

Congratulations for successfully marketing yourself. The company is going to make a sure-win gamble that you will be a continual success.

NEGOTIATING FACTORS

Your initial salary offer will depend on a host of factors. Here are a few influencing conditions:

How desperately the company really wants you

The close parallel between your qualifications and your new job's requirements

Your potential for making the company more money

The company's prebudgeted salary for a specific position and attached benefits package

Current financial problems in the company

The industry's current economic state

The geographic location of the business market

Depending on your specialized skills, you may be offered comparably more or less salary that you are presently earning. If you are an

111

air force aviator rated for piloting C-141s and C-5As, and your next job will be flying for a major airline, then expect to take a hefty step-up on the economic ladder to over $73K. But if you are a separating quartermaster commander and your new job will be a forest ranger, then expect a considerable step-down to about $19K. Remember that the company is paying for your future contributions to the company and not necessarily for your past achievements.

As you compare job offers and salaries, remember that the same job with the same firm, performed in different parts of the country, will fetch different salary offers. For example, you may be paid less, and spend less, working and living in Georgia than in Manhattan simply because of the significant difference in cost of living. Other considerations include local competition, market saturation, and public demand for your services.

As a general rule of thumb, ask for a salary that is between 10 and 20 percent above your current salary. However, this rule is generally applicable to civilian-to-civilian jobs. Depending on your military specialty, you may have to accept an initial significant decrease in wages.

Before the negotiation begins, discretely determine the salary paid to other employees in the same position. This will provide you with a good starting point. Always check several sources and compare notes because the figures may vary due to differences in seniority and information accuracy.

The simplest technique for obtaining salary data is to ask an inside source from your web of networkers. Another method is to exploit those intelligence assets you developed earlier while hanging out at the employees' favorite lunchtime and after-work places. Also, a safe technique is simply to phone the payroll section, anonymously identifying yourself as a prospective employee. Say you are considering working for the company, but would like to know the salary range before making any decision.

THE BENEFIT PACKAGE

During the negotiation process, always discuss the additional benefits. Remember not to expect any benefits unless you specifically ask for them. The company is attempting to preserve its funds; the less you request, the more they keep, and the better the interviewer appears in the eyes of his boss for saving the company money. The following is a partial list of some possible benefits and compensations:

Relocation expenses (moving, hotels, and closing costs)
Commissions and bonuses
Business account for meals, travels, and entertainment
Cost-of-living and inflation salary adjustments
Overtime, nights, weekend, and holiday pay
Company car
Tuition assistance
Retirement account
Paid vacations and unpaid off time
Medical and disability insurance
Injury and sickness compensation
Family medical coverage
Dental plan
Children's day care (for the single parent)
Elderly care (for the child provider)
Profit sharing
Stock options (owning company stocks)
Paid sabbaticals (for independent research)
Use of company legal and medical services
Exclusive office rights or personal work space
Space-available travel on company transports
Employee shopping discounts
Free samples of company's product
Club membership
Severance pay
Outplacement employment services for your next job

Determining Comparable Value

If, during the negotiation, the topic of your current military salary is raised, remember to provide your total compensated salary figure.

This amount includes all your service benefits, including the following:

Basic pay	Medical care
Quarters allowance	Death and survivors programs
Subsistence allowance	Social security coverage
Variable housing allowance	State and local tax advantages
Incentive and special pay	Reenlistment bonus
Overseas allowance	Retirement plan
Hazardous duty pay	Paid leave and holidays
Family separation allowance	Education programs
Clothing replacement allowance	Base services and entertainment activities
Federal tax advantage (nontaxable allowance)	Assistance programs (Welcome Closets, emergency aid)
Commissary and exchange savings	Space-available MAC travel benefits

Review your Personal Statement of Military Compensation, released annually in February. Check your local finance office for a personalized current edition. This will provide an accurate reflection of your actual earnings in the event your potential employer wants to know your present pay and benefits.

No Guarantees

As you have discovered, our modern military did not guarantee you permanent employment. Budget deficits and the perceived reduction of a future threat are eliminating the need for hundreds of thousands of defense positions. Without a need, there is no demand.

The same can be said for any civilian occupation. In a few short years, your intended career field may vanish, replaced by technological advances or outpaced by society's needs.

It is to be hoped that you will select a new profession, one with longevity—at least for your lifetime. Therefore, you must preview your career path within the company. Critical features to consider during any negotiation are promotion opportunities and salary reviews.

In any profession, you want to feel the gratification of advancing in your career and see the visible fruits of your progress. Promotions and pay raises are essential elements for the psyche and the pocketbook. Review them sensibly before finalizing your agreement.

Long-term versus Short-term Goals

Remember the childhood story of the race between the tortoise and the hare? Recall that the speedy rabbit expended all his energy in a mad dash for the finish line. He quickly became exhausted and lost the race. But the determined tortoise progressed slowly but steadily forward, one positive foot after the other, and eventually won the race.

The moral of the story is to consider your short- and long-term goals. Evaluate the possible future benefits of jobs that start at lower salaries but come with pledges of steady pay raises and promotions verses jobs with higher beginning salaries but with limited growth potential. Take into consideration if and when you plan to make additional career changes and the rising cost of inflation.

Do not accept or reject any offer too hastily. Remain in control and request a day or two to consider the offer. Interestingly, most job offers occur on Friday, giving you the weekend to think it over. Ironically, most job terminations also happen on Friday, no doubt to reduce the trauma for both the terminator and terminated.

SIGNING THE CONTRACT

Anticipate that some companies do not formalize their employment agreements with any written contracts. Instead they rely on an old-fashioned "gentleman's agreement." If you are dealing with a long-standing reputable firm, this type of agreement may be perfectly acceptable.

Consider requesting a formal written contract if you suspect personnel layoffs are imminent, if the agreement is complex, with many assorted benefits and promises, or if there is a history of contract disputes. A contract will protect both your rights and privileges and ensure that all parties understand their obligations.

If you request or are offered a contract, be sure that the following items are adequately addressed:

Job title	Commissions and bonuses
Job description	Reporting relationship
Term of employment	Contract and salary reviews
Starting salary	Severance pay
Benefits and incentives	Transition services

Congratulations! Your long pilgrimage is almost complete. Time to take that well-deserved vacation, regain tranquility, reenergize your spirits, and finally put away this book.

But if the thought of a regimented company life-style just does not appeal to you, at least for now, if you feel more comfortable wearing blue jeans than power ties, if you want to be your own boss, if you have the urge to spread your wings and soar to new heights, then read on.

═══ **CHAPTER 13** ═════════════════════════════

THE ENTREPRENEURIAL SPIRIT

Thinking about striking out and starting your own business? You are not alone. Each year millions enter the the self-employed small-business world. Unfortunately, thousands hang up a Going Out of Business banner in less than two years. Your success as an entrepreneur will depend on your forethought and prudence.

AN AMERICAN TRADITION

The invitation read: "Give me your tired, your poor, your huddled masses yearning to breathe free. . . ." And they came. Streaming in by the hundreds of thousands from every distant shore. Guided by "The Lady's" flickering flames and a dream, America offered freedom, opportunity, and a bright future. The streets filled with the symphony of exotic tongues. Despite language barriers, assorted customs, and near poverty, they succeeded. Their dreams live on in their college-educated sons and daughters. The privileges and opportunities are now yours. The future generation is yours.

Your achievements, like theirs, will be the product of extremely long hours of hard work, imagination, and perseverance. To help determine if you are actually suitable for the rigors of starting your own business, I recommend that you read the following books:

The Entrepreneur's Complete Self-Assessment Guide, by Douglas Gray (Fortuna, Calif.: ISC Press, 1986).

Small Time Operator, by Bernard Kamaroff (Laytonville, Calif.: Bell Spring Publishers, 1988).

Avoiding the Pitfalls of Starting Your Own Business, by Jeffery P. Davidson (New York: Walker & Co., 1988).

Entrepreneur's Guide to Starting a Successful Business, by James W. Holloran (Blue Ridge Summit, Pa.: TAB Books, 1987).

Once again, this is only a small sampling of the many fine books available. The federal government also offers two free booklets for veterans interested in starting, financing, and managing a small business:

More Than a Dream: Running Your Own Business (Washington, D.C.: Department of Labor, 1981).

Veteran's Handbook (Washington, D.C.: Small Business Administration, 1989).

The Small Business Administration (SBA) provides preference to veterans in obtaining assistance. Although they cannot make direct business loans, they can help guarantee loans made by banks and savings and loan associations. For more information, contact your local office of the SBA, listed in the Blue Pages under Federal Government. The SBA has a very helpful program called the Service Corps of Retired Executives (SCORE), an excellent source of useful information and business contacts.

THE NECESSARY STEPS

If you have already determined your enterprise, than continue with your desires. But if you are still uncertain about what you want to do, here are some suggested paths to your next guidepost.

Determining Your Business

Remember the commercial, "Let your fingers do the walking"? Leafing through the Yellow Pages is a simple and rewarding way to get ideas for a new business.

Review the phone book for specific areas where you are interested in starting your business. Count the number of like advertisements offering the same product or service. This is a perfect indicator of how much competition you will face on the open market and where the competitors are located.

Drive down any major highway, through any city. Look around and take copious notes about prospective businesses.

Visit stores that interest you. Walk through as a customer and browse. Develop a sense for the business. Notice how many customers there are, how the store is laid out, how business is conducted. Talk to the manager and salespeople. Most will tell you the trade's good and bad points. Some may even offer inside suggestions and lessons they have learned. Be careful, some owners may downplay the market if they realize you are going to be another competitor.

Visit several businesses and compare. Be sure to visit at various times to compare activity levels.

Consider taking a part-time job in one of these stores. This is an excellent way to obtain a good feel for the business. This exposure may provide you with a sample of the trade's less-attractive features.

Visit your local library and review trade magazines and product publications.

Include your family throughout this selection process. If your family is like that of most new small business owners, your spouse will be your new faithful business partner and your children the semifree labor force. Also consider including other interested family members, especially the ones who may already be in the business. Their intimate expertise is invaluable.

Deciding your new vocation may be the easiest part of your transition, especially if you already have a strong hobby interest that you want to transform into a full-time endeavor. Once you have zeroed in on a prospective enterprise, ask yourself these four questions:

1. "Do I have enough skills and knowledge to start and run this business?" If not,

2. "How do I receive the right training?"
3. "Do I have enough seed money to start this business?" and
4. "Do I really have a burning passion to see this business succeed?"

Once you are satisfied with your responses, you are ready for the next step, the examination of your finances.

Start-up Expenses to Consider

Depending on your selected business, the financial requirements will vary considerably. A simple example: opening a restaurant will cost substantially more than starting a small consulting firm.

Your initial outlay will also vary significantly. For example, starting a business from ground up will cost substantially more than buying an existing one. Purchasing a present business by yourself will cost more than entering a partnership. And a partnership may be more expensive than taking over a family business.

The costs of purchasing a franchise will differ appreciably. Some items to consider: cost differences between companies providing the same product, your level of participation, associated costs of property purchases, training fees and geographical marketing rights. Like any smart shopper, look around and compare prices before buying.

Develop and analyze your own financial profile by consulting with an accountant, a lawyer specializing in small businesses, and someone from your bank's business loan department. Be prepared to discuss your general business ideas and marketing strategies (what and how you want to sell).

Include in your assessment your ability to meet both business start-up and sustainment costs. Do not forget a reserve fund to meet emergency needs.

Project how much additional revenue you must budget until your business breaks even and becomes self-sufficient. It may be several months or years after opening day before you actually earn a profit after expenses.

It's time to pause for a mental break. The trek up money mountain may seem an insurmountable task, requiring Herculean strengths, the Forbes family's wealth, and Donald T's showmanship. But many have reached the summit and looked out on the glorious majestic panorama. From the peak, all paths lead downhill to the lush green valley.

Starting your own business will be a long and arduous journey, filled with many hazards and challenges. The rewards will be great, but only for those who dare to take the risks. More trivia: the late Malcolm Forbes was an infantry army staff sergeant during World War II.

Finding a Business Place

Location, location, location—those three words sum up your potential for success or failure.

Consider the advantages and disadvantages of each location you visit. It will be very helpful to convert the information given below into a personalized checklist for note-taking. For those hot prospects, I recommend taking along a Polaroid camera for a quick snapshot; pictures will come in handy later when you are ready to sort it all out.

For simplicity's sake, imagine operating a new business in your own building. Mentally image your own location and means of ownership. As you read on, you will discover the pros and cons of owning or renting a building, sharing a business place, or operating from a shopping center or mall.

The following is intended to stimulate your business mind.

Apply the same principles to inspecting a business site that you would apply to purchasing a new house. For the many readers who spent most of their career living on base, purchasing a new home will be an eye-opening experience. But here are a few business pointers to consider.

First check the building's overall condition.

☐   Examine all sides of the structure. Look for obvious defects and repair problems. Check the roof's condition. Ask the realtor to find out how old the roof is. If it's more than 15 years old, consider eventual replacement costs.

☐   Inspect the interior on all floors. Check the ceiling and walls for necessary repairs, or for modifications needed to support your equipment and display materials. Examine the types, number, and locations of your windows. Consider possible renovation costs if they don't complement your intended work arrangement. For example, if you are opening a gallery and picture-framing shop, you may want specific types of display windows to highlight your work but need to guard against the damaging effects of the sun's ultraviolet rays.

☐ Test all features. Check to see if the electrical system is adequate for your needs. A machine shop will require upgraded voltage capacity, whereas a lamp fixture store will need more outlets. Check the plumbing system. A laundromat will require additional plumbing connections. Consider customers' rest room facilities. Check the heating and cooling systems.

☐ Check the fire codes for your type of business. The condition of the structure, required safety modifications, the distance to the nearest fire hydrant and station will all have an impact on your fire insurance costs.

☐ Space is an important consideration. Ample space will be needed for working, storage, office, display, waiting areas, and parking.

☐ Beware of major defects. Hire a professional building inspector to provide an estimate for the cost of completing all major repairs. Add the contractor's estimate for any necessary remodeling. Include the expenses for mandatory safety corrections. Then add a reasonable percentage increase for the many "unexpecteds."

If you detected many undisturbed cobwebs, a November 1963 calendar on the wall, or original Coca-Cola glass bottles on the windowsill, assume that the building has been unoccupied for awhile. Check with the realtor for the date of last occupancy. More importantly, talk with the neighbors about how it was occupied.

Identify your primary clientele that will patronize that location. Will your business be for corporate accounts, residential customers, small firms, or off-the-street consumers? Consider the following:

☐ **Off-hour business.** What is the marketability of your trade after 5 P.M. and on weekends?

☐ **Neighbors.**   How close and what types of business neighbors will you have? What do their storefronts look like? Will they help attract or detract customers for you?

☐ **Neighborhood.**   Take a long walk through the area, do not just drive through. Only by walking will you actually capture the neighborhood's unique character. Get out and meet the people; they may be your future customers. Do you see faces of despair or happiness? Look at the maintenance and upkeep of the buildings, sidewalks, and vacant lots. Develop a feeling for the community's sense of pride and economic future.

☐ **District.**   Is the area improving, stagnating, or deteriorating in appearance and business?

☐ **Competition.**   Where are your closest competitors? How much of a threat will they be?

☐ **Proximity.**   What and where are the locations of other high-volume businesses? Remember, many customers have grown accustomed to the "park once and shop" concept.

☐ **Visibility.**   How easy will it be to see your store from a distance? This helps new customers to find you and others to be enticed by your display and publicity signs.

☐ **Accessibility.**   Once they know where you are, how easy will it be to reach you? Busy intersections of main streets and thoroughfares are often best for variety stores and minimarkets.

☐ **Trafficability.**   How much vehicle and pedestrian traffic is circulating through the area? The more people, the better your opportunity for more customers.

☐ **Parking.**   Is ample parking space available? Is there free public parking? Or will customers have to pay for garage or off-street parking? Customers will drive right by if there are no safe and conveniently close parking areas.

☐ **Handicap.**   Is the store accessible to those who are in wheelchairs? Does the parking lot have designated parking spaces? Are there special entrances and exits? Elevators? Are facilities such as water fountains, washrooms, aisles, sales counters, and check-out stands user-friendly?

☐ **Noise.** How noisy is the area? Depending on your trade, you may prefer a quiet tranquil working environment, or a roaring, congested area.

☐ **Security.** How safe is the neighborhood to shop in? Will customers feel safe visiting you after dark? How secure will your premises be after you lock up?

☐ **Resale.** How much, if any, profit will you make when you decide to sell your business?

I hope these suggestions will be useful guides, possibly triggering other new ideas. The intent is to whet your appetite to learn more and improve your preparedness, to realize your fantasies and not stifle your dreams.

BUYING A FRANCHISE

If you are not ready to tackle a business alone, then seriously consider owning a franchise outlet. Depending on the franchise you select, much of your support, planning, training, and expenses will be shared by the owning corporation. You will still be the local boss and reap a share of the profits.

In a franchise operation, you will be exchanging a portion of your operating independence for the security of corporate support. Attracting customers may be slightly easier, because people are more comfortable in dealing with a well-known firm.

Many major corporations are very selective in whom they permit to own or operate a franchise outlet. Most require successful completion of their training course, participation in a nonpaying apprenticeship program, a *substantial* initial investment, and assignment to a preselected marketing area (possibly across the country).

Being a franchiser will definitely require more than a nine-to-five commitment. Invest your time and money wisely in an industry that truly appeals to you. A good means of comparing business opportunities is to attend several business-opportunity trade shows.

One such fair is the International Franchise Association exposition. The association sponsors trade shows 12 times a year throughout the country. Contact the managers, the Blenheim Group in Orlando, Florida, at (407) 647-8521 for the next fair date in your area.

Remember the story of the charlatan consulting firm in Chapter 10? *Be aware that fraudulent franchise schemes are also multiplying at an alarming rate.*

At open trade shows and expositions, some bogus promoters have been known to set up their advertising booths next to reputable franchises (for example, McDonalds or Minuteman Press). This is a familiar con-artist technique to project legitimacy and suggest investment security. Look out for "ringers," convincingly talented, but dishonest actors who act the roles of successful franchise owners.

Here are some safety tips. For any franchise, always demand to see a copy of the company's financial disclosure statement and Uniform Franchise Offering Circular. The latter is a mandatory, comprehensive 23-item prospectus that lists financial and legal information for initially starting one of their outlets.

Always visit several *fully* operational franchise sites. Ask a lot of questions. Return later when the "usual salesmen" are not around. And never sign any agreements without first consulting with your lawyer and accountant.

The following two books will help you decide if franchising is right for you:

The Complete Handbook of Franchising, by David D. Seltz (Reading, Mass.: Addison-Wesley, 1982). This is an excellent all-source book detailing feasibility, financing, advertising, training, and operations.

The Source Book of Franchise Opportunities, by Robert E. Bond (Homewood, Ill.: Dow Jones-Irwin, 1989). Another superb reference guide listing virtually every known licensed franchise categorized into over 50 business specialties. The book provides current summaries of each franchise's headquarters, history, finances, training, and support. It also contains an extensive bibliography on franchise publications.

Regardless of whether you decide to own or franchise, permit me to offer, at no extra charge, some practical business wisdom. Your five keys for opening a small business filled with success:

1. Select a business that provides services or products in popular demand both today *and* tomorrow.
2. Find a good location.
3. Provide your customers honest, courteous, and prompt service. Always market quality merchandise at a reasonable price.
4. Treat your employees with decency and pride. Show that you really care about providing a safe, clean, and happy workplace.
5. Work hard, be patient and your perseverance will lead you to prosperity.

I hope your Going Out of Business banner will remain stored away until your grandchildren retire.

The next chapter furnishes some useful advice on how to prepare your family for that next big upcoming event—moving.

CHAPTER 14

THE LOGISTICS

Moving can be a dream or a nightmare. It all depends on what you are leaving and where you are going. Regardless of whether moving brings you pleasure or pain, the following lessons learned will improve your planning and preparedness.

PACKING AND MOVING

You have a distinct advantage if you are already firmly established in a civilian community and have opted to remain in place come separation day. Your familiarity with the area and employment prospects should benefit your job search.

For those who want to, or must, move, then here are a few suggestions. Begin planning at least three months before the movers arrive. If you intend to make major purchases from the post/base exchanges, carefully evaluate your budget situation and future Green Card shopping privileges.

You may discover bargain sales on furniture after arriving in your new community. The less you have to pack and move, the fewer headaches for you and the family. But if you do decide to buy, then do it early.

Avoid any last minute purchases because those deliveries may be delayed, thereby upsetting your scheduled pickup date and departure schedule. If you are planning to continue service in the Reserve, remember you can always make purchases during active duty periods.

Itemize and segregate those items that you will continue to need during your travels, en route vacations, family visits, and job searches. A few extra copies of your résumé may come in very handy when visiting your network of families and friends.

If you are planning to integrate personal visits with business searches, be sure that you pack accordingly. Depending on your profession, some old clothes, work boots, a notebook, camera, binoculars, and measuring tape may be useful.

For easy access later, pack separately your new career transition tools: business clothing, answering machine, personal computer, résumés and cover letters, dictionary, copies of all your service and medical records, and other reference items.

Its best to be pessimistic. Plan, pack, and carry as if this were going to be a very long job search. If you are planning to store your household goods until after you locate your new job and home, remember to carry and not store appropriate clothing for all seasons, cooking utensils, and entertainment items. Avoid having to repurchase items you already own while temporarily staying in motels and apartments.

Arrange in advance to have a friend or family member serve as an interim communications point to which your requests and phone calls may be directed while you and the family are on the move.

Expect up to *five weeks'* delay in delivery of forwarded mail. Prevent missing that golden interview opportunity by indicating a moving date and forwarding phone number in your applications and cover letters. Consider advance rental of a post office box at your future transient site.

For those in search of temporary or permanent quarters, consider contacting local realtors for housing reports about your different destinations. Many realtors are linked to a nationwide computer network of apartment and housing information.

You may also contact several promotional agencies for free guides and magazines. These illustrated publications are excellent ways to size up the areas' housing market (availability and costs).

Homes & Lands Magazine
Homes & Lands Publishing Corporation
P.O. Box 5018
Tallahassee, FL 32314
Tel: (800) 277-7800

Condominium & Apartment Guide
Apartment Directories & Guides of America, Inc.
14304 Chaparell Place
Tampa, FL 33625
Tel: (800) ADA-RENT

HOUSEHOLD GOODS

You are entitled to have your personal belongings, within your weight allowance, shipped at government expense back to your original "home of record"—that location where you first entered active duty.

If you plan to settle down in that quiet little town a few miles from your record home, you must negotiate your requirements with the transportation office and not the commercial contractors. Some moving firms have set distance limits beyond which they will charge an extra fee. Here are two examples to clarify the point.

☐ Say you entered active duty in Honolulu, are presently moving from the Fort Dix and McGuire Air Force Base area in New Jersey, and are planning to settle in Colorado Springs. You are entitled to have your household goods shipped back to Hawaii. Although your destination is Blue Sky country, you will not incur any additional charges because you are within your authorized distance allowance.

☐ If you entered the service in Fayetteville, North Carolina, are moving from Camp Pendleton in California, and retiring in Coral Gables, Florida, then you are entitled to shipment back to North Carolina. However, you must pay the extra expense of shipping your goods on to Florida because you exceeded your distance limits.

For those of you who have no firm destination yet, relax. Uncle Sam will provide free storage of baggage and household effects for up to six months. For those involuntarily separated, storage time is extended to one year, but no longer. If you need extra storage time, contact your transportation office. Be prepared to reimburse the government for any additional storage expenses. Always work through your transportation office and not the movers, because any changes must be government approved.

To authorize a final delivery address and date, you must *personally* visit the Joint Personal Property Shipping Office (JPPSO) or Transportation Management Office (TMO) located on any military installation. Keep this in mind, especially if you are planning to resettle in a distant and remote area.

Remember to bring all your documentation, including your separation orders detailing you to your original transfer and separation point. Those orders contain the necessary moving accounting codes.

A new DD Form 1299, Application For Shipment and/or Storage of Personal Property, will be prepared and sent to your originating JPPSO or TMO. They, in turn, will dispatch release orders to the contractors. Your local JPPSO or TMO will then let you know on what day the shipment *may* arrive. Of course, you should contact the movers to coordinate a final delivery time.

Plan in advance to expect up to several weeks' delay between visiting your local TMO and receiving your final shipment, especially if you had several separate shipments. It is not uncommon for household goods stored less than 50 miles from your destination to take six weeks to arrive.

Do a thorough and complete postdelivery inspection. You are still entitled to file claims against both the carrier and the U.S. government; obviously you can collect from only one. Your nearest military installation's claims office should be able to help settle any claims.

You will have up to 70 days to inspect your property and record all losses or damages. Your DD Form 1840, Joint Statement of Loss or Damage at Delivery, must be delivered to a local claim office not later than 70 days from your delivery date. Submit it any later and you risk a reduction in the collectable amount. Finally, you have two years from delivery date to file your claim against Uncle Sam.

As mentioned earlier, Congress and the Pentagon brass are still debating additional benefits for those involuntarily separated. Among the proposals was the following: allowing separated personnel to rent their present government quarters for up to six months and free storage for up to one year. Check with your separations and transition office for approved benefits.

The next chapter is a hodgepodge of interesting and helpful facts, advance knowledge that will give you an insider's edge on taking advantage of the benefits that you have earned and deserve.

CHAPTER 15

A POTPOURRI OF VETERAN BENEFITS

MEDICAL CARE

Take advantage of all preseparation medical screening and treatment opportunities, especially if you are not retiring with benefits. Obtain free quality medical care, such as physical examinations, eyeglasses, X-rays, and prescriptions. Consider the tremendous amount of money these services would cost if you were to obtain them in the civilian sector. Also remember to schedule your examinations as early as possible in the event that further tests or follow-up treatment will be required.

As a veteran separating before retirement and having any service-related medical or compensated dental conditions, you may still receive treatment at most military medical facilities. The Veterans Administration (VA) will also provide hospital or outpatient care when needed to treat those conditions. Treatment will be provided at your local VA medical center or clinic. Under specific circumstances, the VA may pay for outpatient care given by your family doctor or dentist; however, the VA will not authorize payment for any services not approved in advance.

If you are retiring, you and your dependents remain eligible for receiving free health care at many military hospitals and clinics on a space-available basis. This is an important point to consider when deciding where to resettle, especially if you or a family member require chronic medical care or specialized therapy. Note that under the present CHAMPUS program, retirees under the age of 65 still have the option of receiving treatment at participating CHAMPUS medical facilities.

Service-Connected Disability

The VA will also provide you hospital care if you have any rated service-connected injury, that is, a disability by injury or disease incurred or aggravated during active duty service while performing in the line of duty. The treatment of service-connected disability is also extended to the following veterans:

Certain administratively discharged (under other than honorable conditions) personnel

Active duty retirees for a disability incurred or aggravated while in the military service

Those with an income below $16,466 and without any dependents

Those with a spouse having an income below $19,759 (add $1,098 for each additional dependent)

Veterans receiving a VA pension

Those eligible for Medicaid

Former prisoners of war

Those exposed to certain dioxins, toxic substance (i.e., Agent Orange) while in Vietnam between Aug 5, 1964 and May 7, 1975

If you are being discharged from active duty because of a service-connected disability, you may also be eligible for other VA benefits: compensation payments based on the severity of disability, an increased allowance if the VA rates you as being 30 percent or more disabled, vocational rehabilitation training, dependent's educational assistance, clothing allowance if you use prosthetic or orthopedic devices, and assistance in obtaining tax exemption on a portion of your retirement income.

Nonservice-Connected Disability

The VA will also provide hospital care, on a space-available basis, to veterans with the following nonservice-connected disabilities, that is, a disability not incurred or aggravated during active duty service:

Veterans with an income between $16,467 and $21,954 who have no dependents

Veterans with an income between $19,760 and $27,443 who have a spouse (add $1,098 for each additional dependent)

Veterans with an income exceeding these amounts who pay the VA an agreed-upon copayment

You can obtain a free dental examination and all appropriate treatment up to 90 days after your discharge, provided you have not already receive any final dental care within 90 days prior to your separation. Both your on-base dental clinic and local VA hospital can provide you these services.

In addition, the VA will provide dental care at any time, to the following veterans:

Those with service-connected compensable dental disability

Veterans with service-connected disability rated at 100 percent

Veterans with service-connected noncompensable dental disability, that is with a combat or service injury; or former POWs (with less than 90 days in captivity)

All POWs with more than 90 days in captivity

Contact your local VA representative for more information on other veteran benefits to which you may be entitled. Check often, since VA policies and eligibility requirements are occasionally revised.

INSURANCE

On your discharge day, you will be given the opportunity to convert your Servicemen's Group Life Insurance (SGLI) to Veterans Group Life Insurance (VGLI). If you elect not to continue your coverage, the Department of Veterans Affairs will mail you a notice, application form, and information pamphlet about one month later to reoffer you this opportunity.

A not-too-well-publicized fact is that *your SGLI protection contin-ues through the 120th day after separation, without any additional monthly contributions.* And if you are totally disabled at the time of separation, your protection continues for one year, or until the day your total disability ends, whichever comes first.

The extended coverage for total disability is not automatic. You must notify the Office of Servicemen's Group Life Insurance (OSGLI), and provide medical documentation to substantiate your total disa-bility. The address is:

Office of Servicemen's Group Life Insurance
213 Washington Street
Newark, NJ 07102-2999

Inform your spouse, family, and other beneficiaries about this ex-tended benefit. In the unfortunate event of your death during the coverage period, they may file a claim by contacting OSGLI. They must also provide a copy of your DD Form 214, Certificate of Release or Discharge From Active Duty, and a copy of your death certificate.

Take time to review your family's interim insurance needs and medical coverage, especially if you are planning extended travels to visit relatives and friends, or are scheduling extensive job-hunting campaigns in various cities. Additional insurance protection may be necessary to cover your travels, property in transit, personal property, and temporary rental property.

Remember your SGLI and VGLI are both term life insurance. There is no cash value or interest payments, and you cannot use it as collateral for a loan. But you may not find any other term life insurance with lower premium costs than VGLI. The VGLI is a five-year policy, convertible at expiration to a commercial policy.

If you elect to convert SGLI to VGLI, you have 120 days from your separation day to apply without providing proof of your insur-ability. After 120 days, you must provide medical evidence (physical examination documenting your good health). Important note: your application rights permanently expire within one year and 120 days after separation.

The Survivors Benefit Plan (SBP) is a separate government-sponsored life insurance program for all retirees. Upon separation, regardless of your health or insurability, you will be given the option of continuing in this program. If you elect to participate, an automatic allotment will be deducted from your monthly pension check to pay your premium fees. In the event of your death, your surviving spouse or dependents will continue to receive up to 55 percent of your monthly military retirement pay.

If you are married and decide not to participate in the SBP, or desire less than the maximum coverage, your spouse must also provide his or her written consent. Without SBP coverage, your retirement pay will cease on the day of your demise. You and your family should carefully consider the merits and demerits of this program, because once you enroll it is virtually impossible to modify your coverage or cancel your policy. You would be wise to shop around and compare costs and coverage benefits of other substitute plans, or to augment SBP with an additional commercial policy.

EDUCATION

Improving your education will always benefit your future and can even expand your employment opportunities. As a veteran, you may be eligible for educational benefits under one or more of the following government programs:

☐ **Noncontributory GI Bill.** This is the familiar old GI Bill that expired December 31, 1989. However, you may still qualify for benefits by transferring your eligibility to the current Montgomery GI Bill. To be eligible, you must have served a continuous period of 181 days or more of active duty, between January 31, 1955, and before January 1, 1977, and also served three years of continuous active duty after June 30, 1985. The required 181 days does not apply to time served as a cadet or midshipman at a service academy or while assigned to attend a civilian educational institution.

☐ **Post-Vietnam Veterans' Educational Assistance Program (VEAP).** This was the voluntary contribution program whereby the government matched $2 for each $1 you invested in VEAP, with a maximum total individual contribution of $2,700. This program affected those entering the service after December 31, 1976. You will be able to use your benefits up to 10 years after your discharge; an extension may be granted if you are disabled. Your maximum entitlement is 36 months, or the number of months of your participation, whichever is less. You may also request a refund of any unused contributions.

☐ **Montgomery GI Bill.** This is the current program for veterans who entered the service after June 30, 1985, and elected to contribute $100 (nonrefundable) a month for their first 12 months of service. Your eligibility for these benefits will end 10 years after discharge, but may be extended because of disability. Basically, you must have served three years of continuous active duty to be entitled to 26 months of benefits. Serving an additional five years will increase your benefits to 36 months.

Program Options

The VA provides many other educational and training programs, such as farm cooperative training, apprenticeship, on-the-job training, and tutorial assistance. The VA also offers the Work-Study Program for full-time students using their veteran's education benefits. This program gives you an additional money allowance (not less than minimum hourly wage) for working in a VA office or project. You may work up to a maximum of 250 hours per enrollment term and up to a maximum 750 hours per year.

You can use your VA benefits to attend many types of education or training courses, including colleges, refresher courses, night classes, apprenticeships, correspondence schools, language training, and specialized programs. Taking night courses or weekend classes may even help ease your transition back to civilian life, and assist you to relearn the art of being a student.

Campus Life

If attending college is your next step in life, consult with your academic counselor to determine if any of your military training can be applied towards college credit. You may be eligible to take certain College Level Examination Program (CLEP) tests for undergraduate credit without actually attending classes.

Most graduate schools will require you to first successfully pass the Graduate Record Examination (GRE) or other special tests, such as the Graduate Management Admission Test (GMAT). Remember, each school has its own minimum acceptable test scores and standards of acceptance for admission; you may be rejected by one school and be accepted in another.

If you are contemplating law school, you will be required to score sufficiently on the Law School Admission Test (LSAT), which is administered four times a year. Applications are available by writing:

The Educational Testing Service
LSAT Office
Princeton, NJ 08540

To help you prepare for these examinations, many commercial self-help manuals are readily available in libraries and bookstores. Avoid outdated manuals by checking their publication dates; you will find that most current editions are available only in bookstores.

Maximize your awareness of all available educational benefits that you are entitled to as a veteran. *Remember that knowledge is knowing where to locate the information you are seeking.* For starters, consult with your base education counselor, college finance officer, VA benefits counselor, alumni representative, and academic advisor. Hundreds of thousands of dollars in valuable scholarships and research grants remain unused each year because people did not learn about their availability.

SECURITY CLEARANCES

Prior to separation, you should receive a final security debriefing and sign an acknowledgement letter. At that session, it will benefit you to review DOD Pam 5220.22M, *Personnel Security Clearances*. This pamphlet should refresh your memory concerning your ongoing security commitments and responsibilities.

Remember to request a copy of your current DD Form 873, Certificate of Clearance and/or Security Determination. You may need this for your new job.

Many major federal agencies (for example, the Federal Bureau of

Investigation and Drug Enforcement Administration) will not fully recognize your DOD clearance and will require you to undergo their own screening program. Anticipate an additional wait of from three to nine months before actual employment. Your investigation may take even longer, depending on the level of clearance required, the extent of your foreign travels and connections, and personal problems.

Your employment opportunities may also be limited in some agencies (Central Intelligence Agency and Defense Intelligence Agency) if you are presently married to a foreign national. If your valuable talents are critically needed, they may grant an individual waiver; but do not rely on any quick approval.

Some civilian defense contractors may accept and convert your valid Department of Defense personnel security clearance into an industrial security clearance. You have up to 12 months from separation day to request a conversion. If you are retired with 19 or more federal service years, than you have up to 18 months. For specific details, contact your potential employer's personnel security office.

IMPORTANT RECORDS

During your outprocessing, be sure to make complete copies of all your important government documents. It is essential that you keep entire copies of your medical, dental, and personnel records. These papers will be invaluable when you apply for VA benefits, receive any medical care, enlist in the National Guard or Reserve, or file a legal claim or medical lawsuit. In addition, you should obtain copies of military training records, diplomas, transcripts, and awards.

Be wise and safe by also making copies of all your essential civilian documents, including your current will, character reference letters, personal medical records, eyeglass and drug prescriptions, dental and physical X-rays, children's school records, contracts, and operator licenses. Consider mailing the originals to a trusted relative or friend and using copies during your travels.

Prior to separation, visit your local office of the Judge Advocate General for any necessary legal assistance (e.g., powers of attorney, wills, and notary). Of course, if you are retiring you will continue to be eligible to receive these free services.

Before setting out, remember to obtain an ample supply of all prescription medications. Have copies of your prescriptions readily available in case of emergencies and to give to your new doctors.

DD Form 214

Your Certificate of Release or Discharge From Active Duty, DD 214, is an extremely importance document, an everlasting testament of your military service. Upon separation, register your original DD 214 with your county or state register of deeds office. Request a certified copy for future use. The VA will only accept a certified copy when you apply for benefits. Ask your separation center to send a carbon copy of your DD 214 to your state's commission of veteran affairs.

Carefully review your DD 214 before signing it. The information it contains will affect your future veteran and educational benefits.

One of your last official acts is to exchange your green ID card for your discharge certificate. Remember to also surrender your dependents' cards. If you are planning to travel on terminal leave prior to your actual discharge date, a temporary card may be issued showing your actual separation date. Upon expiration, you must then mail in your invalid ID card. If you are retiring, you will be receiving your well-deserved blue retirement card.

Obtaining Copies (SF 180)

If in the future you discover that you need a copy of any document in your official service or medical records, then complete Standard Form 180, Request Pertaining to Military Records. This form is obtainable at any Veteran Assistance Center and through many veteran organizations. Reduce response delays by thoroughly completing SF 180 instead of sending a letter. If you do send a follow-up letter, be sure to include the following information:

Full name (as shown on your records)
Service number
Date of birth
Branch of service

Dates of service
Home of record
Place of discharge
Rank upon discharge
Specific description of requested document(s)

Forward your completed SF 180 or letter to:

National Personnel Records Center
Military Personnel Records
9700 Page Boulevard
St. Louis, MO 63132

A replacement discharge certificate (not DD 214) will not be reissued. If your original certificate is lost, stolen, or destroyed, you must send a completed SF 180 to the above address. Instead of a replacement certificate, you will be issued a Certificate in Lieu of Lost or Destroyed Certificate of Service, Discharge or Retirement.

Official Corrections

If you detect a gross error in your military records, or decide to formally protest an injustice, attempt to have the problem resolved before you separate. The longer you procrastinate, the less likely you are to initiate a change. With time, memory fades, priorities change, interest declines, records get lost, and witnesses move away.

Always use your chain of command to mediate any mistake or grievance. If you have exhausted all your available, practical, administrative, and legal remedies, then consider seeking relief at the DOD or secretariat level.

To docket a case for consideration by an appointed review board, complete DD Form 149, Application for Correction of Military Record Under the Provisions of Title 10, U.S. Code, Section 1552. These forms, along with the appropriate regulations, can be obtained at your local staff judge advocates office or personnel center.

The time limit for filing an application is within three years after discovery of the error or injustice. It may be filed by you, your heir, or a legal representative.

LICENSES AND REGISTRATIONS

Each state has its own grace period until you must exchange your driver's license and vehicle registration. Contact the state motor vehicle or police department in your new community for specific requirements before your driving privileges are affected. Some almanacs also contain tables showing time limitations; look under the category of motor vehicle requirements.

RESERVES AND NATIONAL GUARD

If you are considering the option of joining the Reserves to continue your patriotic contributions, you may have to wait. In view of the current downsizing of our military forces, the state reserves and militia are also significantly affected. Some states now have waiting lists for future reservists and guardsmen. Factors influencing how long you wait include the needs of regional units, federal and state budgets, and your occupational specialty.

The events in the Middle East may have a moderate impact on reversing the original force-reduction plans. What type and how much of a change remains to be announced as of this writing.

If you are really interested in a "re-up," check with different units and in neighboring states for job and promotion opportunities. You may have to do a little traveling to make those weekend drills. But considering the number of years you have already invested, this may be a minor hassle compared with the full benefits of a military retirement that you will reap at age 60.

Apply early, if you are considering a return to full-time active duty as a reservist or guardsman. The total forces' downsizing will reduce the number of Active Guard and Reserve (AGR) slots and increase the competition for Reserve promotions. Specific application and selection procedures vary from service to service, but you may expect the following (or similar) competition process each year.

Each year selection boards convene to select applicant officers and NCOs for available AGR positions nationwide. Application deadlines are normally in the spring, with selection announcements being made prior to the new fiscal year. Assignments are filled year round when openings becomes available.

The AGR Selection Board reviews each application packet, which generally consist of a Request for Active Duty form accompanied by recent copies of an efficiency report, personal data records brief, full-length photograph, and other required documents.

Selected applicants are placed on a waiting list by order of merit and occupational specialties.

Once an AGR position in your specific skill becomes available, the top-ranked person in that skill is offered the position. If the offer is declined, that person's name is moved to the bottom of the list and the next person is offered the job. The list is valid for one year and does not guarantee actual placement during that year.

Depending on your standing on the list and the availability of jobs, you may be in for a long wait. To improve your chances of selection, *apply for open positions using one of your alternate specialties.*

Annual reapplication and competitive selection are necessary until you are selected and accept a position.

Assignments are often available at various reserve centers, state armories, recruitment offices, and active installations. A recent congressional amendment eliminated active-duty reservists and full-time National Guard members from being assigned duty with a unit of the Reserve Officer Training Corps program. This change is tentatively scheduled to take effect at the beginning of fiscal year 1992.

Telephone various reserve centers in your adjoining states to ascertain available vacancies. Some small centers are best staffed on weekends.

INVOLUNTARY SEPARATION

The following section highlights some of the transition provisions contained in the current National Defense Authorization Act. Contact your career counselor for more and revised information. These are required services that must be made available to you. Exercise your rights and demand them when necessary.

☐ Mandatory individual preseparation counseling to include educational assistance benefits, vocational rehabilitation benefits, procedures for affiliating with the Selected Reserves, job search and placement assistance, job counseling for your spouse, medical and dental coverage, counseling on the effects of career change, financial planning, and financial planning assistance

☐ Authorized separation pay for officers and enlisted personnel with six (possibly five) or more years of service (not in their initial enlistment term or obligated period)

☐ Repeal of the current $30,000 separation pay limit

☐ Possible requirement for individuals receiving separation pay to become or remain a member of the Ready Reserve for three years from separation

☐ Certification of acquired civilian-applicable job skills and experiences

☐ Employment assistance centers on selected installations

☐ Personally authorized release of your name and credentials (and your spouse's) to prospective employers and employment agencies

☐ Preference for hiring in DOD nonappropriated fund agencies; also available to your dependents

☐ Employment and training assistance program, including labor market information, civilian workplace requirements and opportunities, résumé preparation, job search, interviewing techniques, local assistance programs, loans and grants, and geographic relocation information

☐ Continued medical and dental care for 120 days (60 days for those with less than six years of active service)

☐ Availability for purchase of conversion health policies, including dependent coverage

☐ Continued use of military family housing for not more than 180 days; rental fee to be charged but may be partially or fully waived in cases of hardship

☐ Relocation assistance for overseas personnel

☐ Authorized excess leave (not more than 30 days) or permissive temporary duty (not more than 10 days) to job and house search

☐ Preference for filling vacancies in applied-for Reserve and National Guard units

☐ Nontemporary storage of baggage and household goods for not more than one year

☐   Continue enrollment of certain dependents presently attending DOD dependent schools until the end of their enrollment period (or until high school graduation for those dependents in or entering the 11th grade)

☐   Opportunity for certain personnel to enroll in the Montgomery GI Bill

☐   Selection boards to involuntarily separate *regular officers*

A TIME TO REMEMBER

Once you and your new employer "find each other," the contract is signed, the household move is completed, and the family is resettled, then you can finally pop the cork of that well-deserved bottle of champagne. In celebration, you may be strongly tempted to ceremonially burn all of your job-hunting papers, especially your stack of rejection letters.

Dance for joy, but do not destroy your documents. Your files will become invaluable if you eventually have to repeat this job-search process.

Make your future easier, force yourself and your family to write a brief after-action report. Evaluate your transition process and search technique. List your problems, solutions, and lessons learned. Carefully package all your comments, useful notes, and completed files. Safely store them away for possible future use. If nothing more, your memoirs will become an interesting conversation piece for future generations, and may be worth a few chuckles when you are rich and famous.

Regardless of what the future holds, here are some things you always remember:

You are now a veteran, a patriotic alumni of national service.

Be proud of your contributions.

The difficult ordeal is in the transition.

You are a new and valuable member of the labor force.

You have an obligation to *officially express your thanks* to all those people who helped you move forward.

You will soon be in a position to network, assist, and employ others.

Thousands of new veterans are following in your path. Share your new knowledge, guide their way, lend a hand, and *offer them a job*.

The future belongs to you.

A TRANSITION FABLE

You're driving down a deserted road. It's late at night. You're tired and lonely. Larry King slowly fades away as you disappear into the darkness. You've been on this monotonous winding road for what seems like an eternity, going up and down the same hills.

A misty fog begins to shroud the road, and your vision is obscured. Your car's headlights barely illuminate the road. A heavy rain begins to fall. The steady beat of the metronome-like windshield wipers keeps you company; it also could lull you to sleep.

Only the fear of going off the road into oblivion keeps you awake. You try to concentrate. Your head moves closer to the windshield. With squinting eyes you try to pierce the murkiness. Both hands firmly grasping the steering wheel, you remain in control.

You wonder if you are hopelessly lost. Suddenly, you catch a brief glimpse of a signpost ahead. You slow down and brake to a halt. You roll down the car window and stick out your head to read the sign:

Rocky Road Ahead. Prepare for Long Detour.

It is an old marker, silhouetted against the moonless gray sky. It appears to have weathered many storms, yet it remains firmly planted, still providing directions to lost souls.

With that limited guidance, you prepare yourself for a long and perilous journey. Along the way you experience desperate feelings of being lost and delayed in reaching your destination. But many guideposts appear to reassure you that progress is being made.

Out of the darkness glows the warm welcome of a flickering neon sign. It's a rest stop, a place of comfort and shelter, where the sounds of human voices and jukebox music fill the air. You'll rest here for the night to calm your nerves and map out your course for tomorrow.

And so concludes another part of your journey. Pause and refresh yourself within this sanctuary. Enjoy your momentary interlude of peace from the storm.

With the dawn of a new morning comes the reawakened spirit for fresh adventures. You are now prepared for the challenges of the day.

Along your journey you will pass by many Abilene signs, Twilight Zone bars, Peyton Places, and Twin Peaks cafes. Ghost towns from yesteryear will continue to haunt you. Depressed tires and broken parts are inevitable. But with persistence and forward drive you will finally reach your destination. And so continues this fascinating saga called your life.

As an invisible hitchhiker, I enjoyed sharing this ride with you, and hope you understood the metaphors in this epic talc. I assure you that you will remember this story again and again, as you tour the endless highways of existence. Have a safe and happy journey. May your sacrifices be rewarded many times over.

CONCLUSION

Marching into the future as a civilian again can be a marvelous new adventure or a terrifying trauma. With those familiar words we began our journey many days ago. I sincerely hope you found this text to be educational, beneficial, and entertaining.

Rest assured, your journey will be a marvelous adventure, but one punctuated by fleeting moments of terrifying trauma. Successfully applying the knowledge you now possess should prevent, reduce, or eliminate many of your fears of the unknown. Share your newfound awareness and enlighten others.

In the previous 15 chapters you learned the importance of total family involvement. Together you prepared yourselves for an emotional roller coaster ride and psychodrama. You calculated your financial assets and liabilities; developed planning and record-keeping journals; gained better insights into your destiny; decided whether to pursue a new profession in the world of government, corporate business, or self-employment.

You assembled well-thought-out résumés and letters of introduction that best reflected your unique skills and personality. You located the proper sources of employment information, prepared yourself for the many interviews and ultimate discussions of wages and benefits, and finally readied your acceptance and entry into a new life.

Viewed from the grand perspective of years to come, you will remember these troubled times as the "good old days." Enjoy them now and cherish them later.

As you assemble your résumés and pack away your mementos, you will probably recall many fond memories of your career—the good times to remember, the bad times to forget.

Interestingly, we all tend to talk about our dire experiences more than we do the fine ones. Fortunately, with time comes wisdom and the ability to see life from a new perspective, to appreciate the simpler things that come our way.

Soon your new civilian friends will be asking you if being in uniform all those years was honestly worth it, and would you do it all over again. If you do not immediately reply in the affirmative, more than likely you eventually will.

As you prepare to finally hang up your dog tags, I encourage you to think back over your years of faithful service. In retrospect, you, like your predecessors, probably made many unpopular and wrong decisions. Throughout our lives, we can never "always" make the right decisions. But with trust, we hope that the decisions we do make are the best ones possible, decisions based on our optimum judgment of the situation, information available, experiences, and harsh lessons learned.

If you had the power to alter destiny, you might naturally desire a greater influence over a favorable future. As for your past, if you were presented with the same sets of events, I am certain that you probably would do everything exactly the same. You would do it the same because deep in your heart you know that, after taking everything into consideration, you did your very best and never compromised your integrity—an honor you can be rightly proud of.

When America called, you answered. When the War Eagle screamed in the desert, you responded. When the hourglass of peace ran out, you were there to restore freedom and liberate the oppressed.

Only those who have faced the reality of death can truly appreciate the gift of life and liberty. Only then can we truly understand how precious, fragile, and finite both can be.

Be proud of your contributions and achievements. You accomplished your mission and honored your oath. You served our country well and faithfully. You proved your loyalty, discipline, dedication, and patriotism.

In the days to follow, as you stroll through your new community, listen carefully on a late misty night and you will again hear in the distance the haunting sounds of taps being played, echoing reminder of your gallant service to the defense of freedom and the preservation of peace.

Permit me to be the first one to say:

Thank You for Your Outstanding Service.
I Wish You and Your Family
the Best of Luck
in Your New Career and in Your New Lives.

As I contemplated what to write in these final sentences, I recalled my own ambivalence in departing the service. The joyful excitement of facing new challenges was tempered with the sad despair of leaving the Profession of Arms and the dedicated soldiers, sailors, airmen, and marines that I grew to love and honor.

The emotions I feel for the services are best expressed in this excerpt from my final military ceremony. Perhaps you echo these same sentiments:

The Guidon of Command has now been passed on to a new generation of leaders. With it comes the heritage and traditions of yesterday and, equally important, the challenges of what can be tomorrow.

Forty-eight years ago . . . my father . . . was en route to his challenges in central Europe: the Ardennes Forest of France, the Rhineland, and finally a prisoner-of-war camp. Only through the hardships and sacrifices of our ancestors can we gain a deeper appreciation for the human costs of freedom.

I was once taught that to be born into freedom is a birth gift, to live with freedom is a challenge, and to pass freedom onto the children is our responsibility. Now the family circle is complete. It was only fitting and proper for this ceremony to be held. . . .

It is said that you are a very lucky man if in your lifetime you meet that one special person who can alter the course of your destiny for the better. I am indeed that lucky man, for I have met many during my brief tour of duty, from the youngest private, eagerest lieutenant, toughest sergeant, staunchest colonel, wisest sergeant major to the venerablest general. I have learned from them all and consider myself very fortunate, for I am a reflection of their successes.

As I look across this field of green, I see in the eyes of the brave soldiers a fire burning deep within them, a passion to serve.

To the future leaders, I would be remiss if I did not leave with you a few guides to use during your determined quest for excellence.

First, as young soldiers you will undoubtedly make many of the same mistakes that I and your predecessors have made. Do not become discouraged or lose faith. Properly handled, those mistakes can become your stepping-stones to success.

Second, be a freethinker. When the books just do not seem to provide the right answers, call upon your creativity and inner faith for guidance. Have confidence in yourself and your fellow soldiers. Do not forget your NCOs and officers, for they possess a wealth of knowledge and experience.

Third, plan ahead for every possible failure. But do not become so stifled in micromanagement that you lose sight of your objective. Turn every problem into a challenge. Remember, in combat your soldiers do not want managers, they demand leaders.

And, finally, always take care of your soldiers and their families. Set the standards and lead by example.

You are America's new leaders, a rising generation of promise. The torch of freedom is now passed on to you. With it comes the awesome force of power, the balance of life over death, and the responsibility of honor. You are the guiding beacons for a brighter future.

In the words of John Fitzgerald Kennedy, we must be ". . . willing to pay any price, bear any burden, meet any hardship, support any friend, oppose any foe, to assure the survival and success of liberty. . . ."

During my watch, I have only done what was my duty.

And I have no regrets, except for one: that I am unable to continue marching with you as you press onward into the 21st century, because I know of no greater glory, no higher honor, than to have been given the privilege to serve our country.

To the soldiers, the sergeants and the officers, I wish you a world of peace and joyous contentment. May you always be in the grace of God.

Thank you my friends for sharing with me this moment in time. I bid you a fond farewell and final salute. . . ."

CAPTAIN W. DEAN LEE
UNITED STATES ARMY

Farewell Speech
Doughboy Field

MEANS CALCULATION

Source of Monthly Income

	Month 1	Month 2	Month 3
Salary			
Separation pay			
Retirement pay			
Cashed-in leave			
Unemployment compensation			
Interest from savings			
Interest from CDs			
Dividends from stocks & bonds			
Tax refund			

	Month 1	Month 2	Month 3
Collection of debts & loans			
Spouse's earnings			
Dependent's earnings			
Free-lance & part-time jobs			
Gifts from relatives			
Planned sales of property			
Other sources			
Other sources			
Total monthly income			

Monthly Expenses

	Month 1	Month 2	Month 3
Mortgage payments			
Rental payments			
House insurance premiums			
Property taxes			
Association fees			
Electricity & cooking gas			
Heating oil			

	Month 1	Month 2	Month 3
Water & sewage			
Trash collection			
Telephone			
Cable television			
Magazine subscriptions			
Household maintenance			
Outstanding loans			
Interest on loans			
Automobile loan payments			
Auto insurance premiums			
Gasoline & oil			
Auto maintenance			
Family expenses			
Personal taxes			
Emergency fund			
Life insurance premiums			
Child care			
Medical insurance premiums			
Medical & drug expenses			
Groceries			
Restaurants			

	Month 1	Month 2	Month 3
Tips & gratuities	_____	_____	_____
New clothing	_____	_____	_____
Laundry & dry cleaning	_____	_____	_____
Tuition fees	_____	_____	_____
Children's college fund	_____	_____	_____
Club membership dues	_____	_____	_____
Personal expenses	_____	_____	_____
Recreational activities	_____	_____	_____
Charity contributions	_____	_____	_____
Emergency fund	_____	_____	_____
Other expenses	_____	_____	_____
Other expenses	_____	_____	_____
Transition expenses (see Transition Chart)	_____	_____	_____
Total monthly expenses	_____	_____	_____

Estimated Monthly Transition Costs
(And Handy Tax Record After Annotation)

	Month 1	Month 2	Month 3
	_____	_____	_____
Business clothing Suit, shirts, ties, socks, shoes, coats, hats, gloves, belts & accessories	_____	_____	_____
Personal computer Diskettes, ribbons & accessories	_____	_____	_____
Stationery supplies Typing paper, envelopes & business cards	_____	_____	_____
Résumé reproductions	_____	_____	_____
Postage expenses	_____	_____	_____
Faxing & delivery fees	_____	_____	_____
Answering machine	_____	_____	_____
Long-distance phone calls	_____	_____	_____
Subscription fees	_____	_____	_____
Tape recorder	_____	_____	_____
Gasoline & oil	_____	_____	_____
Toll fees	_____	_____	_____
Parking fees	_____	_____	_____
Auto services	_____	_____	_____
Hotels & motels	_____	_____	_____
Business meals	_____	_____	_____
Entertainment expenses	_____	_____	_____
Laundry & dry cleaning	_____	_____	_____
Incidental expenses	_____	_____	_____
Other expenses	_____	_____	_____
Other expenses	_____	_____	_____
Total estimated monthly transition costs	_____	_____	_____

The Balance Sheet

	Month 1	Month 2	Month 3
	_____	_____	_____
Sources of monthly income	(+) ____	(+) ____	(+) ____
Monthly expenses	(−) ____	(−) ____	(−) ____
Last month's surpluses		(+) ____	(+) ____
Estimated available funds	(=) ____	(=) ____	(=) ____

Today's available fund   _____

Divided by average monthly expenses   _____

Equals number of **Months of survival**   _____

SAMPLE RÉSUMÉS

In addition to the dos and don'ts of résumé writing listed in Chapter 7, "Your Résumé," here are a few more useful suggestions:

☐ Customize each résumé to highlight your marketable skills and achievements that are specific for each prospective employer.

☐ Support your objective with related expertise and accomplishments.

☐ Do not use military jargon, acronyms, or abbreviations.

☐ Keep your action one-liners short and concise.

☐ Demonstrate your creative writing style, but not at the expense of the accuracy or completeness of your statements.

☐ Always be truthful. Never compromise your integrity.

☐ Avoid meaningless elaborations and excuses. Too much information is often more harmful than helpful.

☐ Keep your résumé as short as possible. The more white space—wide margins and sentence spacings—the better.

☐ Attractive résumés are more enjoyable to read. Sprinkle in a few eye-catching phrases in bold printing to emphasize your points.

☐ Avoid using the pronouns *I* and *we*.

☐ Complement each responsibility with quantified results. Use numbers: dollars saved, profits increased, resources efficiently used, quality improved, and production increased.

☐ Be realistic in your claims or you may "overqualify" yourself.

☐ Double-check for spelling and typing errors.

☐ Ensure that the listed address and phone number will still be valid at least three months from now. Include a forwarding number if possible.

☐ Upon completing each résumé, place it aside for a few days and then critique it for spelling, grammar, and content.

☐ Reverse roles and pretend that you are the prospective employer. How effective is your résumé now?

Résumés may be drafted using many different formats. You will probably need several tries before finding the format most comfortable for you.

To help reduce your experimentation time, some sample résumés are reproduced on the following pages to illustrate typical mistakes to avoid. Some before and after models are included to highlight the "demilitarization" process. Remember, you are not masking your military career; you are simply translating it into its equivalent civilian corporate counterpart.

Before: A Chronological Résumé
(The typical first-timer's attempt)

PERSONAL: 1LT Michael J. Smith
1422-B Tamarack Drive
Fort Wainwright, Alaska 99701

MILITARY EXPERIENCES: 1988 – present: United States Army
Regular Army Air Defense Officer

Battalion Adjutant (Jul 91 – present, Fort Wainwright, Alaska)
— Principal staff officer responsible for all administrative and
personnel actions.
— Direct assistant to the Battalion Commander.
— Supervised the 1993 Founder's Day Dinner Dance for West Point
alumni.
— Supervised all promotion and award ceremonies.
— Reviewed efficiency reports for completeness.

Assisted S-3 Air Officer (Nov 90 – Jun 91, Saudi Arabia)
— Supervised combat coordination of four Patriot firing batteries.
— Coordinated the battalion's combat readiness programs with
coalition officers from Saudi Arabia.
— Assisted Operations Officer with integrating European-based air
defense units into the protection of Israel and Turkey.
— Unified all training activities with augmenting Reserve
personnel.
— Responsible for organizing and scheduling all air movements.

Air Defense Platoon Leader (Jan 89 – Oct 90, Fort Carson,
Colorado)
— Responsible for the health, welfare, training, and morale of an
ADA Vulcan Platoon.
— Conducted regular inspections to insure combat readiness of all
personnel and equipment.

161

EDUCATION: United States Military Academy, West Point, New York, Engineer Concentration, 1988.

AWARDS: Army Commendation Medal with "V" Device, Army Achievement Medal, Armed Forces Expeditionary Medal, National Defense Ribbon, Overseas Ribbon, Army Service Ribbon, and Parachutist Badge.

LANGUAGE: Semifluent French speaker.

SCHOOLS: Air-Ground Operations School, Airborne School, Air Defense Officers Basic Course.

SECURITY CLEARANCE: Secret.

REFERENCES: Available upon request.

SALARY NEGOTIABLE. WILLING TO TRAVEL & RELOCATE.

MICHAEL J. SMITH
1422-B Tamarack Drive
Fort Wainwright, Alaska 99701
Residence (907) 555-2030
Business (907) 555-7439

QUALIFICATION SUMMARY

A versatile human resources manager, dedicated to
professionalism and motivated towards team achievement. Over
nine years of demonstrated effectiveness in interpersonal
communication and leadership.

* Reduced personnel attrition by 63 percent, saving transfer and
  retraining costs of $204,000 in just 15 months.
* Created an innovative computer-based management technique
  for assigning new employees to designated sponsors and job
  positions, improving overall morale and worker's performance.
* A principled and articulate manager with excellent
  organizational and people skills.

EDUCATION & TRAINING

United States Military Academy, West Point – May 1988
Commandant's List
Exchange Student in France, six months – Jan 1983

ACCOMPLISHMENTS

* Devised an efficient system to track and control efficiency
  reports, eliminating delinquent or lost evaluations.

163

* Created and implemented a unique automatic support system to aid in the narrative awards writing and production of certificates, improving efficiency 100 percent.
* Overhauled entire personnel record-keeping system, centralized processing, reducing redundancy and paper work by 80 percent.
* Received a prestigious Achievement Award from a General Officer for outstanding supervision of a major annual social event for 18 guests and four distinguished speakers.

EXPERIENCE

UNITED STATES ARMY　　　　　　　　　　　　　　1984–present

Personnel & Administration Director (1991–present, Alaska)
Proficient in supervising a staff of 13 office workers responsible for administrative planning and servicing of all personnel actions.

Assistant Operations Officer (1990–1991, Saudi Arabia)
Able to coordinate major crisis management programs. Supervise all social events, media presentations, and special public affairs.

Unit Leader (1989–1990, Colorado)
Responsible for all aspects in the health, welfare, training, and morale of 30 employees.

Cadet (1984–1988, West Point)
Skillfully managed in-processing procedures for newly arrived personnel. Competent in promoting teamwork and group esprit de corps.

RÉSUMÉ

JULIA NIGHTINGALE KROEBER
1313 Sea Breeze Avenue
Pensacola, Florida 32501
Work (904) 555-9482
Home (904) 555-3947

EXECUTIVE MANAGEMENT

OVERVIEW

Twelve successful years in leadership and operational management positions of ever-increasing scope and responsibilities. Characterized by meticulous planning and organization, efficient management of resources, daily motivation of employees, genuine concern for the employees and their families, and guidance of critical projects from origination to completion.

EXECUTIVE MANAGEMENT

Demonstrated technical versatility and talents to: accurately assess a company's weakness and develop a remedial corrective action plan, improve operational effectiveness and increase productivity, streamline office procedures and implement cost-effective systems. Intimate knowledge and hands-on experience with: organizational development and staffing, personnel administration, operations, information and resource management, and logistical procurement.

PROJECT MANAGEMENT

Developed and supervised promotion plans for seven large-scale community projects involving 2,400 visitors, 21 display stands and 43 vendors. Produced numerous public affairs presentations for senior staff officials.

PERSONNEL MANAGEMENT

Managed all office support operations for an average staff of 50 supervisors. Administered personnel hiring, performance evaluations, promotions, disciplinary actions, terminations, and on-site training.

FACILITY MANAGEMENT

Conceived and regulated plant control procedures for improving accountability of sensitive equipment. Redesigned office layout to improve operating efficiency and quality production levels.

EDUCATION

Master's degree in Business Systems Management from The Pacifica University. Bachelor's degree in History. Graduate of several military advance education courses.

PERSONAL

Completed 10 years in the naval service as a Warrant Officer W-2. Top Secret security clearance. Willing to relocate.

After: A Functional Résumé
(Focused with results in efficiency management)

JULIA NIGHTINGALE KROEBER
1313 Sea Breeze Avenue
Pensacola, Florida 32501-4590
Work (904) 555-9482 • Home (904) 555-3947

OBJECTIVE: A challenging and rewarding career specializing in the development and management of organizational efficiency.

BUSINESS EXECUTIVE: Twelve years of international expertise in developing, organizing, training, promoting, and improving operational productivity. Extensive expertise with the implementation of various contemporary management systems.

EFFICIENCY
Streamlined office procedures that resulted in an annual savings of $192,000 in operating expenses for our bureau in Puerto Rico.

Conducted performance studies for our German district office that improved their productivity by 56 percent.

Devised effective accountability procedures for a major Japanese auto plant to recycle surpluses, saving $1,300,000 during a 14½-month period.

DEVELOPING
A cofounder of the United States Navy's Maritime Institute for Organizational Efficiency.

Recruited and developed a staff of eight management specialists to design various new techniques to improve the Navy's operating productivity.

TRAINING   Trained and managed 50 supervisors for a large office complex. The staff then exceeded the performance of all other divisions in the company, becoming the national winner of the prestigious Hudson Trophy for Excellence.

PROMOTING   Organized and directed advertising projects for seven major community events drawing crowds of over 2,400 visitors.

WORK HISTORY   Chief Supervisor, Organizational Efficiency Division, U.S. Navy, Pensacola, Florida, 1983–present.

Management Consultant, International Sales Concord Trading Co., Barstow, California, 1981–1982.

EDUCATION   Master of Science, Business Systems Management, The Pacifica University, Victorville, California.

Bachelor of Arts, Medieval History, Blakemore College, Redlands, California.

Before: A Chronological Performance Résumé
(Overloaded and generically oriented)

Captain Joe Van Johnson
66-A Puget Sound Drive • Seattle, Washington • 98185-0776
(206) 555-0241

EXECUTIVE SUMMARY: Eleven successful years in managerial
and supervisory positions. Described by superiors as a creative,
articulate, natural leader with exceptional organizational,
analytical, and interpersonal skills. Enjoys team work in an
independent, challenging, and rewarding environment. Genuinely
loyal to the workers and the company. A dedicated hard worker in
making any organization a success. Total improvement oriented
and resources conscientious.

SCHOLASTICS: University of Washington, BS Chemistry &
Economics, 1980 (Distinguished Military Student and Graduate).
Awarded Regular Army Commission. Graduate of numerous
advance management and leadership schools and courses.

PROFESSIONAL ACCOMPLISHMENTS:

Author (Aug 91 – present, Washington)
 – **Creative Writing.**   Scripting the book <u>Metamorphosis</u>, a
   comprehensive career transition guide for assisting veterans
   and their families to efficiently reenter the civilian world.
   Free-lance writer with articles appearing in <u>The Wall Street
   Journal</u>.

Commanding Officer (Jun 89 – Jun 91, New Jersey)
 – **Leadership.**   Able to direct a training organization of over
   300 employees with a staff of 18 first-line supervisors.
 – **Resource Management.**   Managed an annual budget
   exceeding $2 million. Capable of administering services,

169

including establishing policies, logistical procurement, on-site training, quality assurance, vehicle & equipment maintenance, managing housing and cafeteria-style feeding.

– **Employee Relations.** Evaluate performance, mediate legal & personal problems, perform promotions, disciplinary actions, and terminations.

– **Systems Development.** Devised transition plans to efficiently realign and deactivate 18 companies of 360 cadre and 4,500 students within a six-month period.

– **Training.** Adept at orchestrating a comprehensive nine-week training program to successfully train over 1,862 new employees over a 22-month period. Capable of expediting personnel screening programs for the early separation of substandard employees. Experience with developing stress-management programs and family-involvement projects to boost morale and enhance production quality.

Operations & Training Officer (May 88 – Apr 89, Republic of Korea)

– **Project Management.** Competent at coordinating and supervising plans for large-scale projects involving over 500 employees, several distant job sites, and many staff agencies.

– **Cost Control.** Analyzed and implemented streamlined procedures for efficiently forecasting, budgeting, and allocating sensitive ordnance valued in excess of $20 million. A subsequent outside audit agency rated the firm as having the best forecasted versus expenditure ratio in the company's history.

Foreign Liaison & Planning Officer (May 85 – Apr 88, Washington)

– **Strategic Planning.** Competent in establishing and nurturing a network of valuable foreign associates. Develop sensitive operational plans and mutual support agreements with foreign governments.

– **Relocations.** Proficient at orchestrating worldwide relocation procedures and multigovernment transportation requirements.

– **International Affairs.** Represented the chief operating officer on numerous foreign diplomatic liaison and fact-finding missions.

—**Public Speaking.** Comprehensive experiences in producing and delivering formal presentations to senior government officials, to include members of the House and Senate Arms Appropriations Committee, the Secretary of the Army, and numerous important foreign dignitaries.

Computer Analyst & Technical Advisor (Jul 82 – Jun 84, California)

—**Education.** Skilled consultant on academic and doctrinal matters. Able to teach a wide variety of subjects to any size of audience and in any type of environment.

—**Analysis/Feedback.** Evaluated the performance of six separate 700-man organizations rotating through a major training center. Quantified their performance using several computer systems to produce customized audiovisual productions documenting their trends and recommending suggestions for improvements.

—**Innovations.** Designed graphic aid cards to enhance training and accountability procedures. Cards were subsequently adopted for armywide use. Author of several field- and office-operating procedures, evaluation guides, and instructional briefings.

Research & Security Officer (Dec 80 – Jun 82, Alaska)

—**Investigations.** Adept at conducting extensive researches and producing timely and accurate reports.

—**Protection.** Able to develop physical security procedures to safeguard personnel and classified information.

—**Accountability.** Originated unique internal control procedures for expediting personnel investigations, doubling the amount of approved security clearances in half the original processing time.

—**Programs.** Initiated on-site education, training, and intelligence projects that were rated the best in the state of Alaska.

MAJOR AWARDS: (2) Meritorious Service Medals, (3) Commendation Medals, (3) Achievement Medals, numerous other domestic and foreign awards.

<u>LANGUAGES</u>: Fluent Cantonese speaker, retrainable in Hangul Korean and Spanish.

<u>ADVANCE EDUCATION</u> (for Defense Contractors): CAS-3, EWC, JINTACCS, NBC, DLI-KOR, CTC, and others.

<u>SECURITY CLEARANCES</u>: Top Secret/SBI/NDPR.

<u>COMPUTER PROFICIENCY</u>: Deannzo Graphic Imager, Digital VT-105, Planetronics Multi-Comm, TSP 2000, STU II/III, KL 42/43, WWMCCS, CPT 8100T/8525, IBM Display Writer III, Zenith Data Systems, PWP 7000LT.

<u>REFERENCES</u>: Letters from senior officials gladly furnished.

After: A Performance Résumé
(Customized for an operations management position)

JOSEPH VAN JOHNSON
66-A Puget Sound Drive • Seattle, Washington 98185-0776
(206) 555-0241

Objective: Management Position in Operations

Highlights of Qualifications

* Orchestrated operations to successfully train over 1,862 new employees during a 22-month period.
* Streamlined management procedures for over $20 million in sensitive supplies, producing savings of over $250,000.
* Extensive travels to the Pacific-rim countries. Developed international operation plans and relocation procedures, vastly improving mutual support with many foreign governments.

Professional Experience

Management Skill
* Effectively managed an annual operating budget exceeding $2 million, always remaining within expenditure guidelines.
* Devised transition plans to efficiently realign and deactivate 18 companies of 360 cadre and 4,500 students within six months. Refined plans were subsequently adopted as a model system for use by numerous other US Army military installations.
* Managed operations of a computerized analysis section that significantly enhanced the operating abilities of six 700-person organizations.
* Originated unique control procedures for expediting personnel investigations, reducing processing time by 50 percent and improving approval rate 100 percent.

Supervision Skills
* Successfully led organizations, from two-man teams to over 318 personnel, in various operating environments.
* Competently directed a training organization with a staff of 18 first-line supervisors. Company continuously won over 30 prestigious high-performance awards.
* Supervised coordination of seven training operations in the Republic of Korea, involving over 500 personnel, several distant job sites, and numerous agencies, resulting in near-flawless continuous operations with no major mishaps.

Communication Skills
* Produced and delivered formal presentations to senior government officials, including members of Congress, the Secretary of the Army, and numerous important foreign dignitaries.
* Author of eight major documents. The most recent publication will be <u>Metamorphosis</u>, a career transition guidebook.
* Presented instructional briefings and training lectures to audiences totaling thousands.

Proficiency
* Fluent Cantonese speaker, familiar with Korean and Spanish.
* Knowledgeable operator of several computer, word-processing, and telecommunication systems.

Employment History
United States Army, Commissioned Regular Army Officer, 1980 to 1991.
* Commanding Officer, New Jersey
* Operations & Training, Republic of Korea
* Foreign Liaison & Planning, Washington
* Computer Analyst & Technical Advisor, California
* Research, Security & Leader, Alaska

Education
* Graduate of six resident advanced management & leadership schools.
* Bachelor of Science, Chemistry & Economics, University of Washington.

ACTION WORDS AND PHRASES

The following action words and phrases will be useful in the development of your résumés and cover letters. Carefully review all categories as many words are interchangeable and usable in other sectors. These are universal problem-solving classes applicable to all professions.

ACTION WORDS

Analyzing skills
Analyzed
Appraised
Assessed
Audited
Clarified
Computed
Conceptualized
Critiqued
Declassified
Defined
Determined
Differentiated
Drafted
Evaluated
Examined
Identified
Investigated
Qualified
Quantified
Recognized
Refined
Reviewed
Screened
Theorized
Translated
Verified

Planning skills
Classified
Compared
Conceived
Developed
Devised
Equated
Formulated

175

Planned

Targeted

Resourcing skills

Acquired

Allocated

Arranged

Assembled

Attained

Authored

Built

Channeled

Complied

Contracted

Contributed

Created

Designed

Disseminated

Distributed

Diverted

Enlisted

Expanded

Experimented

Fabricated

Gathered

Generated

Invented

Obtained

Originated

Pioneered

Prepared

Procured

Published

Purchased

Recruited

Repaired

Retained

Secured

Wrote

Organizing skills

Automated

Catalogued

Convened

Coordinated

Eliminated

Enlarged

Established

Facilitated

Grouped

Indexed

Innovated

Manipulated

Modified

Orchestrated

Organized

Packaged

Programmed

Recommended

Reconciled

Reorganized

Restructured

Structured

Synthesized

Training skills

Coached

Conditioned

Desensitized

Drilled

Educated

Enhanced

Exercised

Guided

Instilled

Instructed

Motivated

Persuaded

Practiced

Regulated

Remodeled

Reshaped

Revitalized

Schooled

Sensitized

Strengthened

Trained

Tutored

Managing skills

Accomplished

Accounted for

Achieved

Adapted

Alerted

Assisted

Assured

Balanced

Budgeted

Closed

Collaborated

Communicated

Completed

Conducted

Convinced

Decreased

Demonstrated

Eliminated

Enabled

Ensured

Exceeded

Executed
Exhibited
Engineered
Expedited
Implemented
Improved
Increased
Initiated
Instituted
Interviewed
Introduced
Maintained
Managed
Marketed
Mastered
Monitored
Negotiated
Operated
Participated
Performed
Persuaded
Presented
Produced
Projected
Promoted

Proposed
Publicized
Reduced
Repositioned
Represented
Resolved
Revised
Sanitized
Simplified
Sold
Solved
Specified
Surpassed
Undertook

Supervising skills
Addressed
Administered
Advised
Approved
Authorized
Chaired
Controlled
Delegated
Directed

Edited
Enacted
Mediated
Moderated
Piloted
Presided
Served as
Single-handedly
Stimulated
Supervised
Validated

List your unique skills

ACTION PHRASES

Keep your one-liners short, clear, and concise. Convey your enthusiasm in all your performance sentences. Complement your achievements with specific examples or quantifiable results. Remember to include some statements in the present tense to highlight those skills that you can use to contribute to the company's success. This will subtly emphasize your future orientation and potential for positive involvement. Creatively redesign, mix and match, and blend your own unique combinations.

"Analyzed problem areas . . . saving $90 thousand in expenses."

"Authored guidebook . . . to improve performance in the workplace."

"Balanced $98 million in resources . . . eliminating waste and abuse."

"Budget limited materials . . . to successfully complete airport construction."

"Conserved valuable resources . . . saving over $20 thousand."

"Create a reference network . . . to improve knowledge sharing."

"Demonstrated technical expertise . . . eliminating fraud."

"Devise novel projects . . . to reduce work stress."

"Evaluate performance . . . to eliminate nonperformers."

"Educated new staff . . . streamlining office operations."

"Initiate problem-solving techniques . . . to quickly end crises."

"Instructed technical class . . . graduating 57 experts."

"Maintained liaison . . . improving communications by 25 percent."

"Modify products . . . to reduce breakage and costly replacement."

"Negotiated foreign demands . . . successfully satisfying all interested parties."

"Organize efforts . . . to improve coordination."

"Orchestrate multi-operations . . . to accomplish assigned mission."

"Plan operations . . . to reduce crisis management."

"Programmed computers . . . increasing accessibility by 42 percent."

"Reorganized staff . . . improving efficiency by 45 percent."

"Regulate control measures . . . to enhance acceptability."

"Selected to represent . . . acting as prime decision maker."

"Headed new program . . . increasing production by 76 units/hour."

"Vigorously pursue new ideas . . . to stimulate company's growth."

"Verify information . . . to eliminate erroneous messages."

"Wrote a career transition book . . . improving the reader's preparedness."

APPENDIX D

SAMPLE DISPATCHES

Interoffice Request for a Letter of Reference

TO: Ltc R. Chenney, Flight Ops
FROM: TSgt W. Dogan, X4545
SUBJECT: Request for Letter of Reference & Recommendation
DATE: 30 February 1993

Dear Sir:

I respectfully request a letter of reference from you to assist in my career transition. At your convenience, I would like to schedule an appointment to discuss any ideas or guidance that you think will be advantageous to me.

To help you formulate the letter, I have enclosed my current resume and job objectives. In addition to a general appraisal of my work performance, I have suggested below some typical questions that most employers are interested in:

- What is your job title and professional relationship to me?
- How long have you known me?
- What job did I perform?
- How was my performance (e.g., intelligence, expertise, judgment, diligence, aggressiveness, imagination, versatility, appearance, communication skills, potential for success, etc.)?
- How was my character (e.g., dedication, loyalty, integrity, responsibility, morality, etc.)?
- Was I able to operate under stress?
- How well did I get along with others?
- Was I honest and upfront?
- Anything else that is special about me?
- Would you consider hiring me?

With your consent, <u>please provide addresses and phone numbers where prospective employers may contact you in a few months.</u>

Please notify me if I can ever be of any assistance to you. I'll leave my forwarding address with your secretary when I stop by to pick up the letter.

Thank you for helping make my transition a little smoother. I'll keep you posted on my success.

Sincerely,

TSgt Dogan

(2 attachments)

General Cover Letter with Résumé to a Company

William David Michaelson
234 Primrose Lane
Marina Del Ray, CA 90290
(213) 555-9898

March 6, 1993

Ms. Virginia Merriwether
Applied International Technology
600 West Algonquin Road
Schaumburg, IL 60195

Dear Ms. Merriwether:

As a future service veteran with over eight years of direct management experience, I am writing to present my credentials for a general management position within Applied International Technology (AIT).

A synopsis of my work history reflects a seasoned, versatile leader with a highly successful record in technology planning, research and development, assembly operations, and resource management.

Although I am new to the civilian job market, I believe my B.S. degree in Technology Management, coupled with my vast interpersonal and organizational skills, will be beneficial to AIT. Some highlights of my significant achievements include:

— Senior managing officer of a $16 million high technology test bed for the Department of Defense. Our project was completed three months in advance, with a cost savings of nearly $1.5 million.

— Organized a 43-man research and development team to test the feasibility of portable reverse-osmosis water purification systems in a desert environment. This project is similar to your new "Klendis Water System," presently under development.

I believe that the basic tenets of management and the principles of leadership are essentially the same whether a person is in a uniform or a business suit — it is the person who must apply them successfully. I am that person. My potential contributions to AIT are limitless.

Please contact me if my credentials are of interest to you. I will be delighted to discuss how you can capitalize on my managerial and leadership talents to further enhance AIT's excellent record in the area of water purification.

Thank you for helping me make a successful transition. For nearly a decade I was privileged to faithfully serve our country in uniform as a senior noncommissioned officer. Permit me now to continue that service as a new and vital member of your talented team of professionals.

I await your invitation for an interview. At your discretion you may circulate my resume to other interested employers.

Sincerely,

William D. Michaelson

wdm

Enclosure

CHRISTINA FONG-THOMPSON
Quarters 6699
Torri Station, Okinawa, Japan
APO San Francisco 99723

April 23, 1993

Mr. John W. Knight, Jr.
McMartin Aero & Naval Systems
1200 Chesapeake Park Plaza
Baltimore, Maryland 21221

Dear Mr. Knight,

This is in response to your advertisement in the April issue of The Naval Officers Journal, seeking a nautical engineer. I am enclosing my resume as an application for that position.

Your ad states that you are seeking an engineer with a minimum of two years' experience, preferably one with a teaching or research background. My recent five-year tour as an assistant professor teaching maritime engineering at the U.S. Naval Academy, combined with my present assignment as a nautical researcher, are excellent credentials for meeting your requirements.

I am scheduled to depart the service late next month, but I will be visiting friends in the Maryland area from May 9 to May 15. I welcome the opportunity to personally speak with you then. Because of the difference in time zones, I will telephone you during the morning of Monday, May 3, to set up an appointment for an interview.

I am looking forward to meeting you soon.

Best regards,

Christina Thompson

Enclosure

Special Note. Until I get resettled, my temporary mailing address after May 12 will be: P.O. Box 3467, Alexandria, VA 22314. You may leave a telephone message with my family at (703) 555-8448.

Thank-you Letter After an Interview

José Alfonso Rodriguez
987 Mojave Spring Plaza
Twentynine Palms, CA 97213

18 May 1993

Dr. Herman Watson
Tri-Star Engineers, Inc.
7531 Wynn Drive
Huntsville, AL 35801

Dear Dr. Watson:

It was indeed a pleasure meeting with you yesterday to discuss employment opportunities with Tri-Star.

I was very impressed with my visit to your operating plant and with the people I met. Your new research project on the X-21 Night Visual Enhancement System (NVES-21) for the M-1C tank sounds like a real challenge.

My three years' experience as the M-1A tank test manager for desert operations would greatly contribute to your project. Also during my recent one-year tour in the Middle East, I learned a host of invaluable lessons using a similar system. As I mentioned in our interview, I am also experienced in managing the necessary resources to implement field testing of the NVES-21.

I have some unique ideas for possibly adapting this system for future use on other armoured vehicles. I think you may be interested in the great potential for expanding this lucrative market. I'll give you a call next week concerning this.

Thanks again for the kind hospitality.

Yours truly,

José A. Rodriguez

LINDA MARY WASHINGTON
Headquarter Company
2nd Personnel Command
APO New York, NY 09402-0102

June 5, 1993

Mrs. Nina Rasmussen
Amador-Philipsbout Associates
846 Steillacoom Way
Tacoma, Washington 98403

Dear Mrs. Rasmussen:

After seven successful years in the service, I am being separated as part of the overall force reductions. I am now available to apply my managerial leadership talents in a new career field.

My best skills are in human relations, especially in personnel recruiting and advertising. I am seeking to pursue a profession that best utilizes these skills. After seeing your advertisement in the Military Times, I would like to engage your free executive placement services.

Please find enclosed my revised resume. You may circulate my credentials to all potential employers. I would appreciate it if you would concentrate your search efforts using these guidelines:

— Professions: promotional marketing or human resources.
— Employment level: management or supervisory.
— Salary range: $30,000 to $45,000.
— Locations: Seattle to Bremerton. No farther than Vancouver.
— Company: Prefer a "Fortune 500" company, but doesn't really matter.

— Special consideration: I have an autistic child (age 8) who requires special attention, therefore I must limit business travel to trips of short (2 to 3 days) duration.

If you are working on any assignments requiring professional marketing skills, please inform your client companies that I will be available to begin work no earlier than August 1, 1993.

Anxiously awaiting your reply.

Thank you,

Linda Washington

INTELLIGENCE SOURCES AND BIBLIOGRAPHY

GREAT BOOKS ABOUT CAREERS

Bernard Haldane Associates' Job & Career Building. Richard Germann and Peter Arnold. New York: Harper & Row, 1980.*

Dress for Excellence. Lois Fenton. New York: Rawson Associates, 1986.

Dress for Success. John T. Molloy. New York: Warner Books, 1984.

Finding the Job You've Always Wanted. Burdette E. Bostwick. New York: John Wiley & Sons, 1977.*

International Jobs. Eric Kocher. Reading, Mass.: Addison-Wesley, 1990.

The Interview Game. John Koran. Chicago: Follett Publishing Company, 1979.*

The Job Belt: The Fifty Best Places in America for High Quality Employment Today & in the Future. Joseph and Amy Lombardo. New York: Penguin Books, 1986.

Jobsearch: The Complete Manual for Jobseekers. Lee Rust. New York: AMACOM, 1979.*

---

*Not currently in print but may be available in some libraries.

191

Look Like a Winner! Lee H. Cass and Karen E. Anderson. New York: G.P. Putnam's Sons, 1985.

Marketing Yourself for a Second Career. Alexandria, Va.: Retired Officers Association, n.d.

The Perfect Cover Letter. Richard H. Beatty. New York: John Wiley & Sons, 1989.

Peterson's Job Opportunities for Business and Liberal Arts Graduates. Princeton, N.J.: Peterson's Guides, 1991.

Peterson's Job Opportunities for Engineer, Science and Computer Graduates. Princeton, N.J.: Peterson's Guides, 1990.

The Professional Job Search Program: How to Market Yourself. Burton E. Lipman. New York: John Wiley & Sons, 1985.

The Resume Catalog: 100 Damn Good Examples. Yana Parker. Berkeley, Calif.: Ten Speed Press, 1988.

Super Job Search: The Complete Manual for Job-Seekers and Career-Changers. Peter K. Studner. Los Angeles: Jamenair, Ltd., 1989.

Sylvia Porter's Your Finances in the 1990s. Sylvia Porter. New York: Prentice-Hall, 1990.

Throw Away Your Resume & Get That Job. Warren J. Rosaluk. New York: Prentice-Hall, 1983.

The Veteran's Guide to Benefits. Ralph Roberts. New York: Signet Books, 1989.

Where the Jobs Are: A Comprehensive Directory of 1200 Journals Listing Career Opportunities. S. Norman Feingold and Glenda Ann Hansard-Winkler. Garrett Park, Md.: Garrett Park Press, 1989.

Where to Start Career Planning 1989–91: Essential Resource Guide for Career Planning and Jobs. Carolyn Lindquist and Pamela Feodoroff, eds. Princeton, N.J.: Peterson's Guides, 1989.

INFORMATION ABOUT MANAGING A SMALL BUSINESS

Avoiding the Pitfalls of Starting Your Own Business. Jeffery P. Davidson. New York: Walker & Company, 1989.

The Complete Handbook of Franchising. David D. Seltz. Reading, Mass.: Addison-Wesley, 1982.

The Entrepreneur's Complete Self-Assessment Guide. Douglas Gray. Fortuna, Calif.: ISC Press, 1986.

Entrepreneur's Guide to Starting a Successful Business. James W. Holloran. Blue Ridge Summit, Pa.: TAB Books, 1987.

More Than a Dream: Running Your Own Business. Washington, D.C.: U.S. Department of Labor, 1981.

Small Time Operator. Bernard Kamaroff. Laytonville, Calif.: Bell Spring Publishers, 1988.

The Source Book of Franchise Opportunities. Robert E. Bond. Homewood, Ill.: Dow Jones-Irwin, 1989.

SOURCES OF COMPANY PROFILES

Career Employment Opportunities Directory. Ready Reference Press, P.O. Box 5249, Santa Monica, CA 90405.

The Career Guide: Dun's Employment Opportunities. Dun's Marketing Service, 3 Century Drive, Parsippany, NJ 07054.

Million Dollar Directory: America's Leading Public & Private Companies. Dun & Bradstreet, 3 Sylvan Way, Parsippany, NJ 07054.

Moody's Industrial Manual. Moody's Investors Services, 99 Church Street, New York, NY 10007.

Moody's International Manual. Moody's Investors Services, 99 Church Street, New York, NY 10007.

Standard and Poor's Register of Corporations, Directors and Executives. Standard and Poor's Corporation, 15 Broadway, New York, NY 10004.

PERIODICALS THAT ADVERTISE MULTI-AREA JOBS

Atlanta Journal and Constitution. 72 Marietta Street, NW, Atlanta, GA 30383. Tel: (800) 282-8790.

Chicago Tribune. 435 North Michigan Avenue, Chicago, IL 60611. Tel: (800) TRIBUNE.

Federal Career Opportunities. Federal Research Service, P.O. Box 1059, 370 Maple Avenue, West, Vienna, VA 22180-1059. Tel: (703) 281-0200.

Los Angeles Times. Times Mirror Square, Los Angeles, CA 90053. Tel: (800) LA TIMES.

National Ad Search. 2328 West Daphne Road, Milwaukee, WI 53209. Tel: (800) 992-2832.

National Business Employment Weekly. Dow Jones & Company, P.O. Box 300, Princeton, NJ 08543. Tel: (609) 520-4000.

New York Times. 299 West 43rd Street, New York, NY 10036. Tel: (800) 631-2500.

San Francisco Examiner & Chronicle. 925 Mission Street, San Francisco, CA 94103. Tel: (800) 323-3200.

Washington Post. 1515 "L" Street, NW, Washington, DC 20005. Tel: (800) 424-9203, ext 6100.

SOURCES OF COMPANY NAMES AND ADDRESSES

AT&T Toll-Free 800 Consumer Directory. AT&T Directory, P.O. Box 44068, Jacksonville, FL 32232-4068.

Business to Business—A Commercial/Industry Buying Guide. The Bell Telephone Company, regionally published.

Yellow Pages Nationwide Edition. P.O. Box 2557, McAllen, TX 78520.

Where The Jobs Are: A Comprehensive Directory of 1200 Journals Listing Career Opportunities. S. Norman Feingold and Glenda Ann Hansard-Winkler. Garrett Park, Md.: Garrett Park Press, 1989.

AVAILABLE FROM UNCLE SAM

Dictionary of Occupational Titles. 4th ed. Washington, D.C.: U.S. Department of Labor, 1977. Supplements issued periodically, the latest in 1986.

Handbook on Retirement Services for Army Personnel and Their Families. (DA PAM 600-5). Washington, D.C.: U.S. Department of Defense, 1982.

How to Get a Job in the Federal Government. Internal Agency Minority Female Recruiting Association. Washington, D.C.: U.S. Government Printing Office, 1984.

Information Pamphlet for Converting Your SGLI to VGLI, SGL. (PAM 74-9). Washington, D.C.: U.S. Department of Veterans Affairs, n.d.

Military Retirees in Federal Employment. Washington, D.C.: U.S. Office of Personnel Management, 1980.

More Than a Dream: Running Your Own Business. Washington, D.C.: U.S. Department of Labor, 1981.

Navy Guide for Retired Personnel and Their Families. Washington, D.C.: U.S. Department of Defense, 1986.

Occupational Outlook Handbook. Washington, D.C.: U.S. Department of Labor, 1990–91 (issued annually).

Veteran's Handbook. Washington, D.C.: Small Business Administration, 1989.

Veterans Preference in Federal Employment. Washington, D.C.: U.S. Office of Personnel Management, 1985.

These publications should be available at your base Transition Center, Civilian Personnel Office, and Learning Resource Center. Many are free ($1 processing fee) by writing:

Superintendent of Documents
Attn: Mrs. S. James
Consumer Information Center-T
P.O. Box 100
Pueblo, CO 81002.

Also request the free *Consumer Information Catalog.*

TYPICAL INTERVIEW QUESTIONS AND RESPONSES

The following are some typical interview questions and sample responses. Each interview session is unique, therefore it is impossible to draft a perfect response for all occasions. With careful thought and a few rehearsals, however, you will build self-confidence to handle the toughest and trickiest questions.

1. **"Tell me about yourself."** This is the traditional opening question, your platinum opportunity to impress the interviewer and sway the rest of the session in your favor. Present with enthusiasm your "canned" response. Keep your comments to about two minutes. A chronological synopsis is easiest to follow, but *do not* give a verbal rendition of your résumé.

Lead off with highlights of your education, followed with a "snapshot" of your military career (title, location, and duties), and conclude with a few significant achievements. Translate your titles into civilian equivalents. Accentuate your special qualities and experiences that are directly applicable to the job. During the answer to this question, the interviewer will be making his or her initial assessment. Remember the earlier story on the importance of first impressions?

2. **"Why are you leaving the military?"** Be forthright about your separation and positive about the service. Some valid responses:

"I would proudly continue to serve, but the Defense Department budget cuts have caused a reduction in all military forces, eliminating many positions and reducing advancement opportunities."

"Just like corporate business, the military can only provide a service when there is an actual need."

"I would like to apply my education, skills, and experiences to advance further in life for myself and for my family."

Avoid all negative comments about previous superiors, stressful working conditions, promotion passover, leadership conflicts, disagreements about regulations, inadequate pay, health problems, and personal problems. You must decide whether or not to reveal any formal disciplinary actions (Article 15s/court-martials).

3.   **"Why do you want to work for our firm?"**   Review your Ideal Company list from Chapter 5. Extract those qualities that this particular company matches and then blend them with your own talents:

"I selected Mercury Electronics because of its fine reputation for producing high-quality products at a reasonable cost. Your advance technology far exceeds any of your competitors. And I want to be part of your rapid growth in the international market, especially in the USSR. I was stationed at the U.S. Embassy in Moscow for five years, so I know the language, the people, and the sales potentials."

4.   **"What are your best strengths?"**   This one should be easy to answer. Select from your long list of attributes a few that best personify your work performance. Illustrate the relationship between your significant achievements and your potential usefulness to the new company.

"The ability to organize is one of my best assets. Given very short notice during the Middle East crisis, I was able to organize 45 people from different agencies into one unified unit. In just four days, we helped prepare 153 cargo containers for sea shipment to the Mediterranean. I think my ability to organize and operate under pressure will be very useful to your shipment company, especially with the competition against deadlines."

5.   **"Do you have any weaknesses?"**   Transform your weaknesses into strengths.

"Yes, I have a few weaknesses, just like most ordinary people. But whenever I detect a weak area, I always try that much harder to remedy it."

"Sometimes I push people a little too hard to get their jobs done, but I do it because I really care about their being successful in their jobs."

6. **"Do you use any drugs?"**   This is a legal question that may be asked. Many companies now require drug screening as part of the employment process.

"I drink a few beers now and then and some wine with dinner on special occasions. That's all. The service is very serious about any illegal drug use and abuse of legal drugs. I hope your company is too."

7. **"Have you ever been fired from a job?"**   If yes, be prepared to provide a plausible explanation:

"The unit experienced a change in rating leaders and, despite my excellent record and noted accomplishments, I was replaced with someone they knew from their previous assignment."

"My section was consolidated into another division and the resulting reorganization eliminated my position."

8. **"Did you ever receive any formal disciplinary actions?"** Again, be honest in your response. Most formal actions (Article 15s and court-martials) are a matter of public record. If you have been disciplined, cite the specific circumstances, especially if it occurred during your youth, and emphasize that you learned from your mistakes. Any attempt to hide major legal problems will only cause you to live in fear of discovery and may ultimately lead to your dismissal. You may be fired not because of your past record but because of your deceitful cover-up.

9. **"How did you like working for your old bosses?"**   Always give a positive response. Even though you might hate one or two of your old bosses, attempt to find some good qualities to mention. People measure your future loyalty to them by your present loyalty to former bosses.

"Major Taylor was a hard-driving boss who demanded perfection. Considering the importance of our missions, I, too, would demand no less than the best from my subordinates."

"Sergeant Major Ortiz never accepted a no-can-do attitude. I think that is why our unit was always the best."

10. "How would you describe yourself?" This is another open-ended question similar to "Tell me about yourself." Review your personality traits and philosophy of management. Develop a positive image of the real you. This response will require some rehearsing to project the proper sincere impression.

11. "What would be your ideal job and company?" Remember from Chapter 5 the "ideal" lists you rearranged to fit your particular preferences? Well, now it is time to review them again. A basic reply would be:

"My ideal job would be one that has a clearly defined objective, one in which I can be challenged in applying all my skills, and one in which I am given maximum freedom to create new ideas for the company."

Consider carefully how you answer this one. Some positions will require a conservative, submissive response, while others will take a more liberal openness. It is imperative that you do your research homework. Consider the job position being offered before answering. Obviously you would not say that you most enjoy working on an assembly line in the city when the job is for a field salesman in the suburbs.

12. "Where do you see yourself in 5 and 10 years from now?" Again review your Chapter 5 wish lists. In your answer, you may want to project your future duty title, responsibilities and, most importantly, your potential contributions to the company's growth and success. Be sincere and realistic in your response. Balance your response between showing your ambitious drive and overzealousness.

"In five years, I picture myself as a section supervisor. With the training that the company will provide me, combined with my work experience, I am confident that our section will produce the best-quality optical disk in the industry."

Be cautious. Confine your answers to your future with that company. Of course you would never say, "Well, I would like to use your company as a stepping-stone to a better job at Sunrise Enterprises." But be careful that you don't imply it.

13. "Can you lead and motivate people to win?" You have a definite advantage over any civilian when it comes to answering this question. Accentuate your leadership skills with specific examples from your vast military experience. Remember to avoid all military jargon. You will be tempted to be long winded in your response, so be careful to be brief, precise, yet thorough. Emphasize how your leadership talents would benefit the company.

14.   **"Why should we hire you?"**   Distinguish yourself by underscoring the "perfect match" between your background and those advertised in the job announcement. You may have already partially answered this question in your cover letter; now is your opportunity to elaborate with energy and make your written words come alive! Be bold and direct. Say you are the best person for the job and why.

"You wanted someone with 5 to 10 years' experience in human resources management. I have 13 years' experience in dealing with every aspect of human resources, from financial management to crisis intervention."

"You wanted someone who could work under pressure. I experienced combat in Grenada and Panama; you can't ask for any more pressure than that."

"You wanted someone who can manage resources or lead people. I have done both! I have successfully managed over $74 million in equipment and led over 500 people in my career."

15.   **"Are you looking at any other job offers?"**   Be honest, but do not volunteer too much information. Exaggerating other offers may enhance your marketability, but it could also jeopardize your chance with this company. A sufficient response could be: "Yes, I am carefully considering all options."

16.   **"This job can't begin to compare with your service duties. Don't you really think you're overqualified for this job?"**   Even though this is probably an accurate assessment, do not let it discourage you. Your success depends on your future achievements, not your past glories. A good response might be:

"My military experience does improve my credentials, yet I don't consider myself overqualified for any job. We should always be opened to opportunities for sharing our knowledge and improving our life. My background only makes me more valuable to your company."

17.   **"Do you have any references?"**   If you developed your reference file as suggested in Chapter 4, your reply to this question will

be affirmative. This is when those letters of reference and recommendation, including those you requested before your separation and move, will come in handy. Have copies available and any updates in names, addresses, and phone numbers.

18.   **"If we gave you the job, when can we see some results?"** Make a realistic assessment of your abilities and compare them with the job requirements. Use your best judgment and provide a reasonable reply. Steer between the overconfident "this week" and the overly vague "sometime in the near future." An appropriate, yet noncommittal, answer may be:

"Given a reasonable time period for assimilating and learning, I am confident that positive results will soon follow."

19.   **"How much salary are you expecting for this job?"**   Be extracareful. Recall the earlier guidance for salary negotiation in Chapter 12. Avoid naming any specific dollar amount at the initial screening interview. If you quote a too-high figure, you may price yourself out of competition. Give a too-low figure, and you may trigger negative signals about your self-worth. Try a little diplomacy:

"I believe my salary should be commensurate with both the unique talents I will be sharing with other employees and the contributions I will be making to further improve the company's successful record."

20.   **"Do you have any questions?"**   You better have. Interest and sincerity for a job are often measured by a person's visible enthusiasm. Your ability to ask insightful, well-researched, and penetrating questions are positive indicators of your seriousness. See appendix G for some suggested questions to ask interviewers. Supplement that list with a few of your own specific questions.

This is the one time during the interview where active note-taking may be well received. Take accurate and complete notes to help you later in sorting and comparing information.

SAMPLE QUESTIONS TO ASK AT JOB INTERVIEW

Save yourself extra work and reproduce this form for each interview. You may record the answers in the space provided between questions.

1. "What will be my primary duties and responsibilities?"

2. "Are there training programs available for me?"

3. "Could you describe a typical workday for this job?"

4. "What are the evaluation criteria?"

5. "Describe the advancement opportunities and promotion requirements."

6. "Who was the best person to hold this job? What made that person so successful?"

7. "What happened to the last person who had this job?"

8. "What new challenges are facing this company?"

9. "Where do you see the company in five years from now?"

10. "How long have you been with this company?"

11. "To what do you attribute your success?"

12. "Do you enjoy what you are doing and do you like working for this firm?"

13. "What do you think are the best and worst things about this company?"

14. "How about the best and worst aspects of this job?"

15. "Are there any major problems I should know about?"

16. "How many people are being considered for this job?"

17. "How would you describe the best candidate for this job?"

18. "What is the next step?"

19. "When will the final decision be made?"

20. "Is there any additional information I can forward to you?"

21. "When can I expect to hear from you?"

22. "I am very confident that I can do an excellent job. Do you agree?"

Add your unique questions:

23.

24.

25.

26.

A BEDTIME FAIRY TALE

Once upon a time you experienced bitterness and resentment that your career was curtailed. But the anger quickly faded as you convinced yourself that your multitalents were in high demand, that dozens of companies would soon inundate you with lavish offers. You remained enthusiastic and optimistic.

Because everything would very soon be in your favor, you pampered yourself and adopted a wait-and-see attitude. No need to hurry; you had plenty of time. Besides, all your buddies kept saying that employers only become seriously interested after you are separated. Even job placement agencies are not concerned until about two months out. So you waited.

You continued to work as usual, but your bosses wondered if your impending departure adversely affected your performance. So they quietly shuffled you to another office where they thought you would do less harm. Overly sympathetic leaders stopped giving you any assignments so that you could have more personal time. Eventually you felt useless and ignored. Thus you bid good-bye to your staff and signed out on leave. Then you could both enjoy a vacation and devote yourself completely to a job search.

Still void of purpose or definite plans, you hastily drafted a single all-purpose four-page résumé—and approved it with solitary objectivity. So what if it was a little long; you were proud of all your military achievements and you wanted to advertise them. Also it was a morale booster to read your wonderful achievements. Energy renewed, you began expending it recklessly in many directions.

Résumés were duplicated on the office copier. Despite poor reproduction quality, you were convinced that the readers would certainly be impressed by the contents. And no need to include any cover letter, your résumé would speak for itself. Excitedly you shotgunned résumés to every known employer.

Every day you hurried home to check the mailbox and answering machine. Nothing. Days stretched into weeks of agonized waiting. You kept busy and worked off your anxieties. Everything that had previously been ignored was now attended to. You reorganized your files and washed your car several times.

Being home all day gradually lost its novelty. Friction slowly increased between you and your less than understanding family. Your life's partner constantly worried about you, the children, the house, and the future. Every day your mate would reexamine the bankbooks and financial statements, calculating over and over the family's finances, fearful that the money would be depleted before you got your next job.

The family tension became almost unbearable, so out of the house you went. The gym staff saw more and more of you. Your running shoes lost more rubber. Your friends began to worry about your unusual behavior. Perhaps you did wait to long to start your campaign.

Suddenly, a month and a half later the responses begin to arrive. Only rejection letters. Your confidence was eroded and self-doubts developed as you were hammered with rejection letter after rejection letter. You figured something must have been done wrong. But there was no time for corrections because separation day was quickly approaching and it was about time to move off base.

You were overwhelmed with separation physicals, outprocessing, farewell parties, and cleaning. Packing away your military mementos was difficult; each piece brought back fond memories. But somehow you muddled through and cleared post. With discharge papers in hand, you were now a veteran and an unemployed civilian!

With an overloaded car filled with worldly possessions, you bravely journeyed into a new world. But you felt like a scared little child starting the first day of school. Approaching the main gate, you sat up straight with erect posture and squared shoulders. Fighting back teary eyed emotions, you proudly exchanged final salutes with the gate sentry. Looking for the last time into the rearview mirror, you watched "home" fade away.

Your temporary visit to the in-laws turned into an extended stay. Everyone encouraged you to relax and just take it easy. More and more unsolicited and fanciful advice was offered. All thoughts were about the good old days.

As weeks multiplied into months, you tried to maintain some semblance of normality. You feared what the neighbors were thinking when they saw your car constantly parked in the driveway. You decided to create a false image by appearing to go off to work every day. Actually you were seeking the safe sanctuary of the public library. There you passed the workless hours under the guise of a beleaguered researcher.

Confused, bewildered, and scared, you became increasingly withdrawn. Feelings of hopelessness, of nothing really mattering anymore consumed you. Sunken eyes revealed your despair.

Your appearance reflected your self-esteem. This was your first opportunity in many years to walk past the barber shop. You permitted your appearance to deteriorate. You shaved less often. You became reclusive and hid behind your facial hairs. You wore the same clothes day after day. Your eating habits were not the same. You substituted vitamins for actual food.

You felt safe in bed. The sleeping world was your sanctuary from an unconquerable life. You were reluctant to rise out of bed only to face another endless, empty day of broken dreams.

You discovered an enjoyable hobby. Gradually you devoted more and more time to it, neglecting everything else—your family and yourself. After a few weeks, even this pastime became unbearable and you became more depressed and confused.

Remembering the many lectures you received and presented on depression and suicide, you vowed not to be its next fatal victim. Progressively you regained the courage to press on with life. With some positive words of encouragement from optimistic family members and friends, you finally saw a brighter tomorrow. Back you went to the drawing board.

After some painstaking soul-searching, mutual decisions were reached on your new profession. A viable action plan was drafted. But you had some catching up to do. Forwarding address and telephone numbers needed to be updated. A lot of serious research had to be done.

Reviewing your great résumé, you found that it didn't look that appealing anymore. Perhaps you should have "civilianized" it so the recipients could appreciate it. You decided to use a word processor to customize each résumé and cover letter, have someone smart proofread it for mistakes, and to spend a little extra for quality copies and stationery.

Carefully you selected some probable employers and sent them personalized presentations. Finally you received several interviews and, subsequently, some very promising offers.

Even though the "right offer" required a few pay steps down today, in exchange you received the opportunity to take a giant leap forward in your career tomorrow.

Several months of patience, persistence, and deliberate, prudent planning ultimately paid off. You and your rewarding job finally found each other.

And you lived happily ever after (well, at least until your next job).

The [End] Beginning!

INDEX